A Pottery Primer

A Pottery Primer

By

W. P. JERVIS

Author of

"THE ENCYCLOPEDIA OF CERAMICS," "ROUGH NOTES ON POTTERY," "A BOOK OF POTTERY MARKS," ETC.

W. P. JERVIS, OYSTER BAY, N. Y.
NEW YORK: THE O'GORMAN PUBLISHING CO., 76 PARK PLACE
Paper Covers, $1.00
Copyright. W. P. Jervis, 1911

Haviland China

is stamped

Haviland France

Additional stamp on decorated China

Haviland & Co. Limoges

PREFACE

THIS little history of the Potters Art, insensibly grew during its serial publication somewhat beyond the scope of a Primer, but I have ventured to retain the title, for it is only intended as an incentive to further research to those who may be interested either in the ancient history of pottery garnished from the most trustworthy sources, or the original matter first here presented.

W. P. JERVIS.

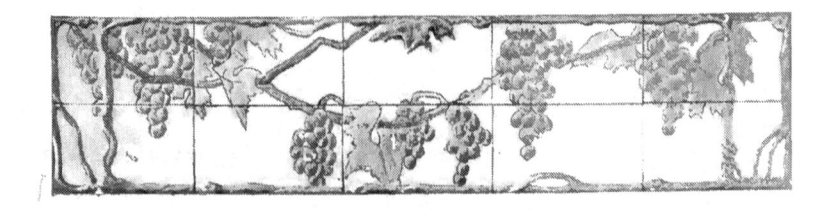

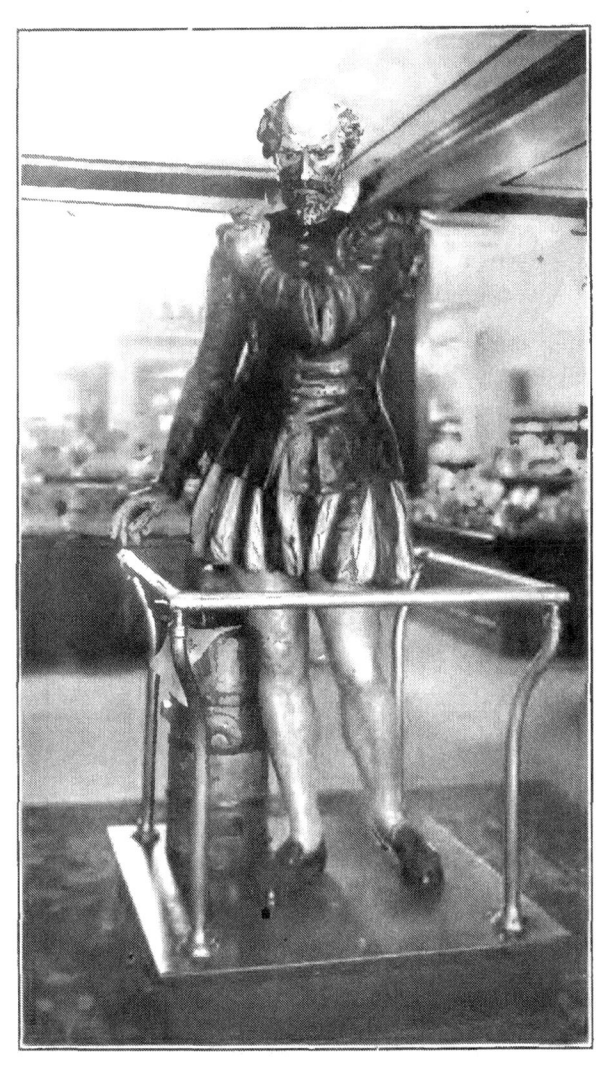

PALISSY THE POTTER.
By Theodore Deck. Courtesy of John Wanamaker, New York.

A POTTERY PRIMER.

CHAPTER I.

NOMENCLATURE.

Let us first try to understand some of the more common terms in general use. First of all comes pottery. There is a regretably restricted use of this word, and it is generally applied to ware that is opaque, as if that was its sole meaning.

It has a much broader significance and is properly applied to any article made of clay and fired, whether a common sewer pipe or one of those dainty Japanese pieces of but little more than egg-shell thickness and so translucent as to be almost transparent. Do not confound these two words, for there is no such thing as transparent pottery.

The word pottery is derived from the Latin word potum, a cup or drinking vessel, and if it had originally a specific meaning it soon lost it as words have a habit of doing and became the generic word for all articles made of clay and fired. Consider in this respect the word potter, a worker in clay, and pottery, a place where pottery is made. No one would dream of differentiating these two words, and they serve to establish the truth of our contention, if any is needed.

The clay and other substances which go to make pottery are known as the body, so according to their quality we have good and bad in a general sense, soft, hard and artificial etc, bodies in a particular sense. The word body well expresses the idea, which may be and has been carried further. The clay represents the flesh, not sufficient in itself, but given the necessary strength by the addition of flint, which represents the bones, and feldspar, because it flows through the other parts, the blood. The Chinese had some such idea, for they speak of the glaze as the flesh and the paste as the bone.

Clay mixtures become pottery only after they have been fired, and if no glaze has been applied, are then termed biscuit.

Perhaps the next most important word is porcelain—a term very much abused, especially in this country. It is a French word used as far back as the Middle Ages, but was then applied only to a shell, similar to mother-of-pearl. In the sixteenth century it assumed a double meaning, and was extended to the newly imported Chinese pottery, and eventually to that of similar character made in France. So, while it has no Oriental derivation, it is rightly applied to pottery of the same composition as that of China, France, Germany, Austria, Copenhagen, etc. It is called a natural porcelain because the glaze and body are made of the natural materials, largely kaolin or china clay and petuntse or china stone. We have used the words kaolin and china clay as synonyms, but it would be more correct to speak of the unwashed clay as kaolin, and as china clay after it is washed and its impurities removed. Kaolin is a decomposed feldspar derived from the decomposition of granite rocks.

In England a more Oriental word was used to designate the English imitation of Oriental pottery, and it was called china, from which we get china clay, china stone, and in Staffordshire they also speak of china works to designate its place of manufacture. When Chinese porcelain was first introduced into Europe its constituent parts were not known, and the chemists experimented with a variety of materials in their attempts to reproduce it. These bodies are classified as artificial, and as such English china ranks. Later we shall see when and under what circumstances European potters were able to make true porcelain. English china is also known as bone china, because bones are used to give it an added translucency and whiteness. There is another point of difference between porcelain and china. In the former case the ware need only be fired the first time hard enough to give it sufficient strength to enable the dipper to handle it with safety, and it does not receive its full fire to insure vitrification until the glaze is fired. In England the body has the hard fire, the glaze a lower one, and in consequence the latter is soft and brilliant. After being for many years a distinctly English production, bone china has recently been made in Sweden, and, of all nations in the world, Japan is now producing it.

Having now determined the meaning of the word porcelain, you can judge for yourself as to what a semi-porcelain should be. Has it a break with an approach to vitrification? Is it translucent, or even semi-translucent? If not answering these conditions, it becomes a trade name only, and should properly be classed as earthenware.

Earthenware embraces all pottery differing from porcelain and china, whether a white or colored body, that is opaque. Tiling, etc., made of a natural red clay is often and properly called terra-cotta, but may with equal propriety be called earthenware.

Faience is an elastic word which has been used to apply to almost anything except porcelain. This recklessness in the use of the word is to be deprecated, because we think there is a distinct kind of pottery which should be so called, and which no other has any claims to We speak of those wares which, to hide the body, are covered with an opaque white enamel. Note here that a glaze is transparent, an enamel is opaque. This opacity is usually secured by the use of tin oxide, hence the name stanniferous enamel. Our contention is this About the end of the sixteenth century the Duke of Nivernais brought to France a number of Italian potters, one of whom, Scipion Gambin, a native of Faenza, settled at Nevers and there introduced the manufacture of pottery coated with a white stanniferous enamel, which had been known to the Italians as early as the fifteenth century It was a revelation to the French potter and became known as Faenza ware, from which the more liquid name of faience was evolved It was a distinct characteristic and worthy of a distinct appellation The Normandy potters were driven out of business by the growth in the manufacture of porcelain and the removal of duty on English earthenware, with which they could not compete. This earthenware had a transparent glaze and in contradistinction to their own faience with it opaque enamel they called it, not English faience, but *terre-de-pipe*, thus emphasizing the name given to this Normany pottery And as simplicity in nomenclature is most desirable, we think the arguments advanced demonstrate very clearly that our definition is correct and should be used only when speaking of wares, such as Delft, painted or otherwise, having a covering of white enamel Majolica is very similar to faience, having the same white enamel, but the true majolica of the Moors in Spain and later in Italy, was enriched with iridescent lusters. The word itself is derived from the island of Majorca where it was supposed to have been made, but this is not so, as majolica in its original meaning was never made in Majorca. Majorca was the port from which the vessels sailed engaged in the trade between the peninsula and Italy, and the ware being carried in these vessels led to its name, exactly as we speak of Lowestoft, because that was the port of entry, not because it was made there, for it was not The fact that the word in Italy has become a generic one for all glazed earthenware need not influence us, nor is its application to colored glazes here and in England of importance, for such ware is best expressed by the term colored glazes, which represents exactly what it expresses

If you will fix these terms and their meanings firmly in your mind, you have already learned much It is worth recapitulation

1 Pottery embraces all clay substances which have been fired
2 Porcelain body and glaze of the same substance · has a vitrified break and is translucent
  (a) English china or artificial porcelain.

3. Earthenware, opaque and not vitrified.
   (a) Faience, opaque, covered with a tin enamel.
   (b) Majolica, the same with addition of lusters.
4. Stoneware, vitrified and opaque.

CHAPTER II.

CLAYS—COMPOSITION OF BODIES.

Before seeing what part clays take in the formation of pottery a few words about the clay itself may be in order.

What constitutes a clay?

Under that general name are included all the rocks or natural earths which, after mixture with water form a plastic body; and harden under the influence of heat.

These clays are formed by the decomposition of rocks by the action of water, their quality and nature depending not only upon the character of the rock, but upon the proportion of pure clay entering into their composition. Of these kaolin is the purest, or rather, is the pure clay, and consists of alumina, silica and water. Kaolin is usually found where the decomposition of the rock has taken place and then always mixed with the rock debris; but sometimes these beds have been displaced with streams of water, which carry the kaolin away until it forms a sedimentary bed. But if the force of the water is sufficiently strong the clay is carried further and in its passage passes over sand, iron, lime, etc., which are carried along with and mixed with it, so that when it is finally deposited a new character has been imparted to it. We thus have sandy, ferruginous (iron) and calcareous (lime) clays, all corresponding in a greater or lesser degree with the two physical properties named in our definition of clay.

So we divide these clays into two classes (1) kaolin; (2) clays properly so called. These latter are divided in turn into three divisions: Refractory, vitrifiable and fusible, and they in turn have their subdivisions.

Refractory clays are such as do not show signs of vitrification when fired to porcelain heat.

Vitrifiable clays which become vitrified at the same heat. If alkaline they are used for the finer grades of stoneware; if ferruginous, for paving tiles, brick, etc.

Fusible clays have the appearance of crumbling earth. They vitrify at a low heat and lose their shape when fired to about 1,150 to 1,200°C.

The plasticity of clay is the result of molecular attraction accentuated by the fact that the grains are very minute and in the form of laminated crystals. By this is understood that the grains are in scales or layers, lying one on top of the other, which allows them to be closer together than if they were spherical or polyhedral, i. e., with many bases or sides

By a few examples we will now see to what extent clays enter into the composition of pottery

Porcelain body.

    China clay 37 27
    Quartz . . .   27 35
    Feldspar 35 36

These proportions may be varied form sixty-five to thirty-five china clay; forty to twenty feldspar, and twenty-five to fifteen quartz.

English bone china:

    China clay 20
    Bone   60
    Feldspar 20

Is not the small proportion of clay remarkable in these two mixtures? Sometimes in the latter the quantity of bones is reduced and Cornish stone and flint added.

Earthenware bodies have unlimited variations ranging from.

    50 to 60 per cent clay substances
    32 to 38 per cent quartz.
    8 to 12 per cent feldspar

The clay substances are usually china and ball clays and almost invariably in England Cornish stone is added

There is the same latitude in stoneware clays, some requiring more, others less, of foreign substances.

M Boutry gives this formula of a German clay

    70 stoneware clay.
    30 China clay
    6 feldspar
    12 flint

Fusible clays to retain their shape and color are fired at 1,200°C

    80 red clay.
    8 china clay
    8 flint

From these formulæ you will see that in no instance is the clay itself sufficient to make good pottery In the last example the clay alone loses its shape and becomes an unpleasant brown color at a heat of 1,200°C, but the addition of the china clay not only strengthens it, but preserves its color and the flint reduces the shrinkage and gives it sufficient resistance to retain its shape and mature at this heat.

CHAPTER III.

PREHISTORIC POTTERY—THE DAWN OF THE ART—EGYPT—INDIA—PERSIA—CHINA—JAPAN.

To know and understand the pottery of to-day you should have more than a rudimentary knowledge of the pottery of the past. It is a delightful study, with romances to stir your heart, with problems to tax your knowledge and secrets to unravel. It is the oldest of the arts; it has been the pastime of kings and princes; the theme of poets; the key to unlock the secrets of the dead past; the story of the ages. It has revealed Egypt, Babylon and Assyria in their zenith; recorded the rise and fall of Greece and Rome, and shown us a civilization in Peru earlier, perhaps, than that of Egypt. It has forced recognition of the learning and knowledge of the Chinese and shown us a civilization there as brilliant as our ignorance was then dense, for which we apparently have never forgiven them. Persia and India it has illuminated too and we know "there were giants in those days." Is it not wonderful to think that a little piece of clay, scratched with a few characters, lost for, not years, but hundreds of centuries, should one day turn up as legible as the day it was made; and be the means of settling some moot point respecting a dynasty but dimly dreamed of?

Written history only tells us that the art existed in prehistoric ages, in "the twilight of the gods." China claims for it an antiquity of two thousand seven hundred years before the present era and asserts it was first practised in the days of the enlightened Emperor Hoang-ti, who was translated to the upper sphere on the back of a huge bewhiskered dragon. Chinese records show that at this time there existed an official known as the Intendant of pottery. Japan credits its origin to a legendary being whom they honored by the title of Kami, distinctive of diety. Egypt to their god Num, or Ptah, the creator of the world, who turned the clay of the Nile upon his wheel, made man and breathed into him the breath of life. Greece credits Vulcan, at the instigation of Jupiter, with making out of clay, Pandora, the first mortal woman. Later, Keramos the son of Bacchus and Ariadne, became the patron saint of pottery, from which we obtain the word ceramic, or keramic. Our own biblical legend makes God the first potter, since he also took dust and made man.

In the pottery of the three nations, China, Egypt and Greece, we find marked characteristics, China beauty of color, Egypt, utility, and Greece the perfection of form.

But undoubtedly the pottery of all people had its origin at the time when they emerged from savagry to barbarism. This presupposes the use of primitive tools and appliances, the desire for necessities and the promptings of nature to supply them. The print of footsteps in clayey ground, which served to retain water; its subsequent hardening by fire made over it; the nest of a bird, and a hundred other causes may have suggested the germ of the idea. Who can tell? The methods employed varied considerably as we know from specimens that have withstood the ravages of time. Sometimes the piece was hollowed out from a mass of clay; sometimes a basket was lined with it and the clay, dried in the sun, separated itself from its mold. But the more general practice was to take rolls of plastic clay and build up the shape desired. It was, at any rate, more desirable than the other two means and enabled the potter to make any shape he desired. Then some heaven-born genius invented the potter's wheel and a rude manufacture was transformed into an art. We do not know when, or by whom, the wheel was invented, Egypt, Greece and Japan all claiming it. We do know that it was used in Egypt four thousand years ago, and that the prehistoric vases of Greece were turned upon it.

The illustration from a tomb at Beni Hassan shows the whole process. Commencing to the left, the first figure is shaping the inside of the cup; the second the outside; the third is taking it off the wheel, while the fourth is putting on new clay. The fifth is making a round slab of clay, and the others are preparing and filling the furnaces and the last one is carrying away the finished product. The illustration shows the wheel in its first stage, turned by hand.

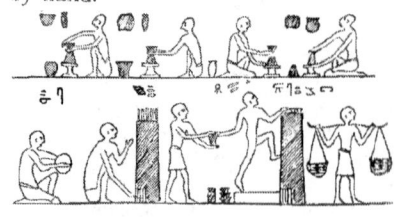

Later, a driving wheel below was added, turned by the foot of the potter; then came the foot treadle, and afterwards the connection of the shaft by means of a rope with a large driving wheel and which remains its approved form, although the majority of those in use to-day are driven by steam. Notice that the thrower uses only the upper part of the clay, a portion being always left on the wheel no doubt on account of the difficulty in centering the clay on a hand-turned wheel. In the illustration of Ptah you will see a change has taken place in the construction of the wheel.

We think it may be conceded that the oldest existing example of human industry are specimens of pottery of a period even anterior to the flint weapons of the stone age. Much of it, crude as it is, appeals strongly to our æsthetic feeling, because there was an evident desire to make the article accurately fitted to its purpose and when this is realized a certain grace of line and proportion must result.

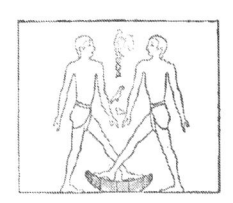

Of the prehistoric pottery of the various races in their earliest strivings to fill their daily wants it is not necessary to dwell at any length and we shall content ourselves with a brief summary. For the beginning one naturally turns to Egypt, Babylon and Assyria, because we have not only the oldest, but the most definite date to start on, for be it remembered that the catacombs of Thebes and Beni-Hassan, on the walls of which are very completely illustrated the processes of the potter's art as then practised, have been proved to have existed nineteen centuries before the present era, and it must have existed long before as shown by the proficiency attained. This pottery was made usually of red clay furnished by the overflowing of the Nile, and the art at a comparatively early stage attained its full development, for the Egyptians had no other clays from which they could fashion finer wares so as to vie with precious metals and stones, and for ornamental purposes clay was discarded. During the first period natural forms were closely followed, for having no predecessors the Egyptian potters had to rely solely upon their creative ability. Afterwards the symbolism of their religion played an important part and we find the scarabæus, lotus, vulture, etc., freely used.

Then metallic glazes came into use. These were but rarely applied to articles of utility, but almost entirely to ornaments for personal use and for tiles for wall decorations. The colors were mostly blue and green, made from substantially the same bases as are used to-day. The body is mixed with sand showing that the Egyptians at this early date recognized there must be an affinity between the body and the glaze, for copper, the base they used, would not produce the turquoise blue on the dense red body previously used.

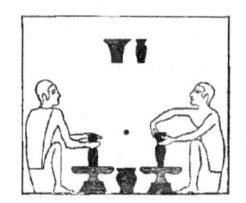

The tablets of pottery of Babylon and Assyria, inscribed with records of their daily life, of their armies and victories; with astronomical observations; of everything else pertaining to their life and country form a magnificent library which even now is far from exhausted and which has been the source of the bulk of our knowledge respecting these countries when everything else failed. There was a whole library of these tablets in Babylon duly catalogued in the same imperishable manner.

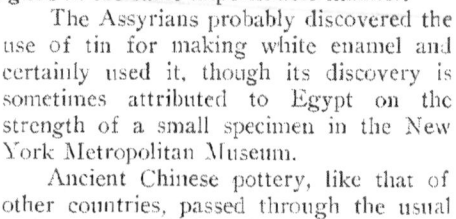

The Assyrians probably discovered the use of tin for making white enamel and certainly used it, though its discovery is sometimes attributed to Egypt on the strength of a small specimen in the New York Metropolitan Museum.

Ancient Chinese pottery, like that of other countries, passed through the usual stages of sun dried and burned bricks, tiles, architectural ornaments, culinary utensils and funeral dishes and vases. It was very similar in character to pieces of Babylonian and Egyptian origin.

Glazes were probably introduced about 200 B. C., and to this period belong the pieces of a rich deep green similar in color to the rind of a cucumber, or the surface of the camelia leaf, and it apparently had a great vogue. These pieces were archaic in form and were modeled after existing designs in bronze. At this early period the body was quite hard. The art seems to have been neglected, but was revived in the fifth century, certain artisans coming from the Indian frontier who introduced into China new methods of making colored glazes.

Pottery was always an important adjunct to Chinese architecture, tiles and slabs of glazed earthenware, or stoneware, being freely used both for inside and exterior decoration. The Porcelain Tower of Nanking, no longer in existence, is a well known example.

India can boast of a respectable antiquity for her pottery, as Hindu writings of the ninth century before Christ make constant mention of earthenware and specimens of red and gray ware, of the type usual to primitive nations over two thousand years old, are in existence.

Persia also yields her ancient treasures as in the ruins of Rhages small unglazed pear-shape pots of a dense stoneware have been found of a date long prior to the present era. And on the site of Susa, which was destroyed by Assurbanupal 641 B. C., glazed and unglazed pottery has been found.

Japan borrowed the art from China. Except for a single reference referring to about 600 B. C., we have no reference to pottery until 29 B. C. There then lived in the province of Idsoumi a potter named Nomui No Sukuné. It was then the custom for slaves to be buried with their dead masters that they might not want for attention in the world beyond. On the death of the wife of the Emperor Suinin this potter made figures of clay and induced the Emporer to bury them with the Empress as substitutes for her favorite attendants. This led to the abolition of the cruel rite and as a reward and distinction the potter was allowed to assume the title of Haji, which signifies "the artist in clay."

This burying of retainers with the dead was also a Celtic custom.

CHAPTER IV.

PERU—GREECE—ROME—MURRHINE VASES.

Before coming to Greece and Rome let us turn aside for a moment and consider a country nearer home—Peru. And at the time we shall consider, Peru included not only what we now know by that name, but a vast country besides extending over two thousand miles south of the equator.

When Peruvian civilization began we do not know, but pottery has come down to us of so remote a date as to make the Incas seem the children of yesterday. These specimens of pottery, from their design and finish, are evidences of a civilization possibly as venerable as the lake dwellings of Geneva, are of the most diverse character and in some particulars resemble Greek and Egyptian pottery. Whether these are the work of that mysterious race, the Chimu, or relics of a still older race, has not as yet been determined.

The road is open here to connect these mysterious Peruvian potters with that equally mysterious race of our own continent, the Mound Builders of Mississippi and Ohio. Many examples of Mound Builders' pottery show a striking resemblance to that of Peru; though not so well finished.

Phoenicia, which embraced the entire eastern shore of the Mediterranean, obtained its knowledge of pottery from Egypt and Assyria. It was imitative rather than creative. Other arts plainly overshadowed it. This great trading and colonizing nation, on the one hand, gave Greece her alphabet, on the other, the ships of Tyre and Sidon reached the shores of England. As to pottery, Greece certainly learned from both Phoenicia and Egypt, but, young and vigorous, she rejected what did not suit her. To the Greek, beauty of form meant everything; color, little or nothing. This expression of form, so perfect is it, has and always will remain a standard of excellence. In grace and proportion it has never been equalled. The potter's wheel was used at least seven centuries before Christ, though the use of molds—made of terra cotta—was not neglected. More primitive pieces go back at least another two hundred years.

We are fortunate in the possession of a wealth of specimens of Greek art, their number in museums and other collections being computed at about fifty thousand. This is owing to the fact that they were all found in tombs, it being the custom to place beside the dead the vessels used in religious rites and the favorite vases of the owners.

It is not to be presumed that Greek art, as exemplified in pottery, was of spontaneous growth. That was gradual and sure from its very commencement until it reached its zenith in the superb specimens with red figures on black ground.

Ordinary common clays were used, but as the art progressed and grew more in favor these were better prepared and made more worthy of the purpose. The earliest specimens are decorated with vertical lines, circles and bands. Then came animal and floral decorations, the drawing of rather a rude kind. Some of these were white on black, while others have the animal figures in dark lines on the red body. Figures in black on red and buff bodies were then introduced and the vases are used as the medium to tell some story of romance, history, or mythology. The flesh of the females is painted white, the drawing is stiff and constrained and occasionally a white slip underlies the black pigment. But in the best art of Greece the colors are reversed, there is more life in the drawing, the figures being carefully and beautifully drawn and the whole is a successful culmination to which previous efforts had led. From 250 to 200 B. C. Greek art began to decline.

MIDDLE PERIOD. BEST PERIOD.

the figures lose their graceful proportion, the drapery is stiff and the ornament overcrowded. Greek pottery entirely disappeared three or four hundred years after the birth of Christ and remained comparatively unknown until the beginning of the eighteenth century.

The shapes were very numerous, the articles themselves being intended for special utilitarian purposes. These included drinking cups, wine coolers, vessels for holding foods and liquors, cooking vessels, water pitchers, vases for prizes in the Olympian games, footed plates, toys for children and receptacles for the ashes of the dead. Many of the vessels intended for food and wine tapered to the base, similar to the bottom of a soda water bottle, so that they could be readily inserted in the sand of the cellar.

It was the rule rather than the exception for the potter to decorate his own product. Of many of these we know the names. Some were potters only, some artists only; a few combined both arts, such as Amasis. Fifty examples of the work of the potter Nicosthenes are known. Cimon of Cleonas (550-500 B. C.) is the first Greek pottery painter we have record of. The celebrated Phidias, Polycletes and Myron all made designs for Greek pottery when in its zenith.

Quite apart from the wares we have briefly indicated are the little Tanagra figures in terra cotta, which, although roughly modeled and made, "convey," as Professor Binns says, "in the most perfect manner all that is essential to beauty." They were small statuettes of gods and goddesses and caricatures of public personages, and were no doubt cherished as the lares and penates of the humbler householders.

Roman pottery, no doubt, passed through the same elementary stages as that of other nations, but largely their inspiration was drawn from the Greeks, though as potters they never equaled them. Distinctively Roman are the pottery lamps, which from the known quantity existing, must have been used very extensively. They were low boat shape, round or oval, usually ornamented with embossed designs and often bear the name of the maker—one in the Jermyn Street Museum has eight burners and formed to be suspended by the aid of three loops. There are two kinds of Roman black ware, one in imitation of the black of Greek vases, but without its degree of perfection; the other, known as Upchurch ware, from its having been found in the neighboring marshes, and dates from the Roman invasion of England, first century before Christ to about the third century of the present era. The black of this latter is caused by the peculiar method of firing, either by the smoke of the kiln or the reduction caused by it of the red to black oxide of iron. It is often decorated with studdings of clay laid on with more or less regularity. Another style of pottery had designs painted on the red body with white slip, the prototype of the delicate pâte-sur-pâte work of to-day.

Much of the interest connected with Roman pottery centers round the slabs and tiles they used so lavishly both for the interior and exterior decoration of their edifices, though these were no doubt the work of Greek artists, the subjects almost invariably being taken from Grecian history. But Roman pottery is usually associated with the fine red Samian ware, so-called because it was originally supposed to have been made at Samos, though it is now generally agreed that the original place of manufacture was Aretium. The body is a red clay approaching the color of sealing wax, and does not appear to be entirely a natural clay, that is, some substance was added to it to reduce its fusibility. This practically accepted fact has only been grudgingly conceded by ceramic writers who find it difficult to credit the potters of the Republic with this important advance in the art. If we take into consideration the ability displayed by the glass makers of classical times, it is only to acknowledge that they must have been skilled metallurgists, and some of their knowledge may have been placed at the disposal of the sister art. Other facts sustain the contention that the body was improved by artificial means. (1) No similar clay has been found, and (2) wherever the conquering hosts of Rome went they must have taken this clay with them, specimens of it, and, more important, fragments of molds having been found both in England and Germany. Much of this Samian ware was quite plain, but a large number of pieces have been found decorated with foliage and ornament, scenes from the chase, games, etc. These were invariably impressed or embossed and finished with glaze so thin as to be almost imperceptible, and which it has been demonstrated within the last few years was formed by a solution of borax.

Some mention must be made of the Murrhine vases, so often alluded to by classical writers, although their composition has never been determined. They were the priceless treasures of Cæsar, Pompey and Nero, and are confusingly described by ancient writers, some indicating a natural substance "extracted from the earth and cut into slabs of small size," others as being "baked in Parthian furnaces." But as no piece, however small, is in existence that can be truly recognized as Murrhine, it remains an enigma which will probably never be solved. The controversy as to whether they were artificial or natural material began in the sixteenth century and has been spasmodically continued ever since. It will be remembered that the Patrician Petronius in "Quo Vadis" before his death broke his Murrhine cup of rainbow brilliancy so that no other should pollute it by touching it with his lips.

The British Museum a few years ago had presented to it a remarkable piece of Roman pottery of which we give an illustration. It is the oldest known example referring to Christianity, and possesses the property that the design appears only when the dish is filled with water. The Chinese have always claimed that they formerly possessed this art, although no specimens are known. This remarkable bowl has in the interior an incised design representing our Lord seated, with his right hand extended and wearing the cruciferous nimbus. On either side of the head are the busts of the Emperor Constantine the Great and the Empress Fausta, and round the top is the inscription, VAL. CONSTAN- TINVS, PIVS. FELIX. AVGVSTVS. CVM. FLAV. MAX. FAVST, which when the bowl was perfect must have begun with + FLAV and ended with A AVGVSTA, so that it would read "Valerius Co(n)stantinus Pius Felix Augustus cum Flavia Maxima Fausta Augusta." The Empress Fausta died in the year 329 A. D., so this bowl must belong to early in the fourth century. It is also one of the earliest examples in which our Lord is seen with a beard and also one of the first instances of the cruciferous nimbus. Formerly there had been no attempt at portraiture, the Saviour being regarded from an ideal point of view, an almost boyish figure with long hair, the type of divine and unaging youth. We have alluded to this as Roman pottery, but it may be Egyptian. From a ceramic standpoint it is a most important piece and has not before been described in this country.

A small fraction of a slab containing part of the Lord's Prayer had up to this time been regarded as the earliest mention of Christianity in pottery.

With the fall of the Roman Empire the potters' art, which had long been declining, disappeared, and though to meet the wants of the people some kind of pottery must have been made for daily use, there is no evidence that anything worthy of being considered an art was kept alive.

This is the first halting place in the history of pottery and we have seen how it was the separate invention of three distinct nations, Egypt, China and Peru, at the beginning of their respective civilizations at too remote an age for us to definitely assign a date. This treasure trove of pottery is of immense value and gives us an insight into the history of nations otherwise impossible to secure. Truly, it may be said of the old potter that he builded better than he knew. Of the existing Hebrew manuscripts of the Old Testament none dates from an earlier period than the Norman conquest, and who shall say what they have suffered in copying and translation from carelessness or ignorance, while the Assyrian tablets and cylinders over three thousand years old tell their story to-day exactly as they told it when drawn from the kiln.

CHAPTER V.
CHINA, JAPAN, MODERN JAPAN, PERSIA, RHODIAN.

Broadly speaking, we have now brought the history of pottery to the commencement of the present era, although, as was inevitable, it has in one or two instances overlapped it a little.

We shall next consider the pottery of China, with special reference to its porcelain, and shall embrace at the same time the ceramic productions of Persia and Japan so as to leave the road open for something like a chronological review of European pottery.

Undoubtedly, Chinese pottery presents the hardest problems to solve that confront the ceramist. The complicated series of marks; the duplication of the triumphs of one dynasty by the potters of the next, not only by native, but also by Japanese artists; the curious figures of ornament; the diverse religions and races, and the complicated written language, all tend to make the subject one to be treated with certain mental reservations.

Thanks to the researches of the eminent Oriental scholar, Dr. Stephen W. Bushell, the author of "Chinese Art," in the admirable series on ceramics issued by the South Kensington Museum, and his catalog of the Walters collection (1899), much previous misconception has been removed. This last work from its high price is not available to the ordinary student, but Dr. Bushell, in collaboration with W. F. Laffan, cataloged the comprehensive Morgan collection in the Metropolitan Museum of Art, and this is published in a cheap form. A study of the collection in conjunction with the catalog would be in itself a liberal education in Chinese ceramics. Where there is diversity of view we have accepted that of these two authors as the last word on the subject.

The Chinese always make a distinction between porcelain and earthen or stone ware, and do not class as porcelain the reddish yellow ware made at Yi-hsing in the reign of Ching-te (1506-1521) or the refractory brown ware coated with colored glazes (Celadon) known as Kuang Yao.

At Khing-te-chen, the great center of Chinese pottery, a porcelain layer was superimposed on the yellowish gray stoneware. Many writers in alluding to this stoneware make use of the Portuguese word *boccaro*. This is not correct, as the buccaros were of Central American, not Chinese, origin, and the word, which had been a general one for drinking vessels in Portugal, was afterwards confined to the scented vessels from Chili. We have no evidence in the form of specimens of porcelain to confirm the Chinese written assertion that it was first made in China during the Han dynasty (B. C. 206-A. D. 25), nor, indeed, for long after that period, and it is open to doubt whether it antedated the Ming dynasty (1363-1643), though a kaolinic body had undoubtedly been made.

In the primitive period which includes the Sung (960-1279) and Yuen dynasties (1280-1367) crackle glazes were perfected, some made by Chang the Elder in the twelfth century having crazes resembling the roe of a fish and called by the French *truitée*. Transformation flambes, the black enamel cups known as Partridge cups; paintings in blue on white were also made during the Sung dynasty, and also the celebrated Lung-ch'üan celadon ware, the green porcelain par excellence of the Chinese, the seiji of the Japanese. It was brighter in tone than the later sea green celadons and the Chinese compared the color to that of fresh onion sprouts. When Chinese porcelains reached France the potters there had never conceived anything like the brilliancy of the glaze and colors and were at a loss for words to decsribe them. A popular novel published in 1647 (who knows that it was not a best seller of the period?) had for its central figure the Bergen Celadon, a fascinating figure of a group of shepherds and shepherdesses who disported themselves in an imaginary world of love and poetry, dressed in silks and gossamers of such tender hues that no commonplace colors could be imagined to correspond with the delicate shades dreamed of by the poets. The Chinese glazes seemed to realize the poets' dream and were so called celadons. This at first applied to all colors, but has now a restricted use, applying only to the gray or sea green tone.

The dynastic colors were of great beauty and the Chinese could find no higher encomium for them than to compare them to jade. This stone is held in the greatest possible veneration by the Chinese. It is a simile of the highest quality of virtue and purity and is an attribute of every meritorious quality. Their

CELADON CUP.

name for it is yu. It is an extremely hard stone, very heavy and of fine grain, and when polished has a beautiful waxy appearance. It varies from white to dark green, though reds and blues are spoken of. To achieve the appearance of jade in their pottery was to obtain an expression of beauty beyond which it was not possible for the imagination to go.

CHIEN LUNG VASE.
COURTESY OF "KERAMIC STUDIO."

During the Yuan dynasty the wares enumerated above were continued, but they lacked the technique and finish of the ware of the previous dynasty. It is to the Ming period that much of the best porcelain that has come to us is usually ascribed, owing partly to the fact that when the Chinese began exporting pottery they thought its age would carry the same added value to us it possessed for themselves, and the bulk of it was therefore antedated some two hundred years. William F. Laffan, in his preface to the catalog of the Morgan collection, says: "Perhaps the most familiar date mark upon the Chinese porcelain so widely distributed in all European countries in the seventeenth and eighteenth centuries was that of the reign of Chêng-hua, 1465-87. Thousands and thousands of pieces of it survive, but we have never seen a piece of porcelain bearing the Chêng-hua mark which was made in the reign of that monarch. We have never seen a piece bearing it that was older than the beginning of the reign of K'ang-hsi, 1662-1722, but we have seen a vast number that

BLUE HAWTHORN JAR.   BOWL OF K'ANG-HSI PERIOD.

were even more modern." During the reign of this last monarch everything worthy of reproduction was counterfeited in a marvelous manner, and to further complicate the situation must be taken into consideration the Japanese reproductions and those of the Chinese of later date.

There is in the Morgan collection a white eggshell bowl and modeled in the paste throughout, but only visible in direct sunlight, are beautifully drawn dragons amid cloud forms and emblems. The paste is translucent and of exquisite fineness. In the disk inside is a mark ascribing it to the period Yung-lo (1403-24). This almost corresponds with the ware mentioned by several old writers, which had the distinguishing characteristic that the design in the piece was not seen until it was filled with a liquid.

Mr. Laffan further states: "The fine reds, the '*Sang de bœufs*,' were all Ming pieces and by a curious fatuity were called *Lang-yao*, a family of potters named Lang being created spontaneously for them. These last were really K'ang-hsi (1662-1722) porcelains, and were Lang pieces in good faith, having been produced under the prefecture of the great Lang, who gave so great an impetus to the art under the protection of the peaceful Tartar monarch." Many beautiful blue and white pieces, the Mussulman blue and the five colored porcelain, green, red, yellow, black and blue of the Ming dynasty, the first four on glaze, the blue on the biscuit,* all look their age; often it is this sense alone that can determine the age of a piece.

The blue, black and green Hawthorn pieces, which are not hawthorn at all, but the blossom of the winter flowering wild plum, or wei flower, do not date earlier than K'ang-hsi, though usually ascribed to the previous dynasty. The blue are the best known, having been made for ginger jars and protected by a netting of stout fiber, were used for the exportation of ginger. The ground of these is broken up into an arbitrary pattern known as cracked ice, upon which is picked out in the white of the glazed surface the flower decoration. The blue is of the most lovely color. The ground of the black Hawthorns was applied on the glaze, as was also the green, though at a harder fire. Sometimes when these green pieces were not up to the color standard a black ground was superimposed on it. These Hawthorn pieces do not date earlier than 1662, and it is doubtful if any pieces of the black and green were seen in Europe before the nineteenth century.

Chinese porcelain has been divided in groups, viz., the archaic, the chrysanthemo-Paeonian, the green and the rose; the celadons, crackles, blues and white being exceptional, so, for example, where green predominates in the decoration it is regarded as belonging to the green family. The want of knowledge at the time this division was made is, we think, its only excuse, for it has nothing in common with ceramics and may safely be discarded.

The chrysanthemum and peony were both largely used and the former was frequently associated with the pheasant, the latter with the fabled phœnix. This association of ideas is carried further, mandarin ducks being usually seen with lotus flowers, wild

---

* . . . . the five colors of Wan-li (1573-1619)

geese with reeds, storks with peach blossom and deer and eagle with pines. But, as we shall see later, the group chrysanthemo-Paeonian really belongs to Japan.

In the K'ang-hsi period (1662-1822) the egg shell porcelain attained perhaps its greatest perfection. It was usual to cover the backs of these pieces with a beautiful rose color, which, reflected through the delicate paste, enhanced their delicacy. These were painted with the utmost care, with figure subjects of the greatest variety.

BLACK HAWTHORN VASE.   K'ANG-HSI VASE.

During this period the painting was wonderful in its variety and beauty, scenes from Taoist mythology, from Chinese history and the more subtle themes of the poets being largely used. The blue in many of the pieces is what is known as "powdered blue," that is, it was blown on with a rude atomizer.

The Grains of Rice porcelain was also made. This consists of piercing the porcelain and then filling up the interstices with glaze, so that the pattern is scarcely noticeable until held to the light.

In the fourth period (1723-1795) the ingenuity of the Chinese potter reached its height, the reticulated vases being triumphs of workmanship. Two vases of this period in the Morgan collection are elaborately decorated with enamels and have outer casings of the body, pierced through with four reticulated panels of foliated outline. These panels vary in design, the first a plain hexagonal network; second, three clawed dragons opposite a tiger in a rocky landscape, and the other two openwork scrolls of bamboo and prunes.

The Mandarin porcelain which Jacquemart erroneously ascribed to Japan also belongs to this period. They were octagonal shape vases, with a cover surmounted by a lion, made familiar to us by the Dutch reproductions. Red was the dominant color and each vase had eight panels, on which were painted Chinese public functionaries. The faces are painted with more care than before, suggesting foreign influence. The dresses are that of the period, the most noticeable features being the toque (a rolled up cap), the short coat and the pig tail.

From this period the art gradually declined and practically came to an end with the Tae-ping rebellion and the burning of the great pottery town of Khing-te-chên. This has partially been rebuilt. From books it is not possible to gain much idea of the value of Chinese pottery, but it has two marked characteristics. The first is the beauty and diversity of color, to match which we must go to nature itself for comparison. The other is its solidity and seriousness. There is scarcely a piece of Chinese pottery that will not impress you with this idea. It is as if the Chinese potter had voiced the words of Henry van Dyke:

"This is my work; my blessing, not my doom;
Of all who live, I am the one by whom
This work can best be done in the right way."

Occasionally you may see references to Chinese soft paste or *pâte tendre*. There is no such thing in the European acceptance of the term.

CHIEN LUNG VASE.

JAPAN.

Japanese pottery owes much to the influence of Corea and still more to that of China. The former seems to have contributed only the method of production, early Corean ware having little to distinguish it from other primitive wares. One of its peculiarities is that in the foot of each piece a small triangular piece is cut out and this is often found in old Satsuma and other pottery of Corean influence.

In A. D. 200 several Corean potters are known to have settled in Japan, and in 463 a further number were brought by a Japanese prince from Petsi, one of the three kingdoms into which Corea was divided. They practically established the pottery at Karatsu (Hizen) about the end of the seventh century; the Raku pottery at Kioto about 1550; another at Seto about 1590, and somewhat later one at Hagi. But the most important was the one at Satsuma, fostered by the princes of that name.

Chinese influence proved more important. Kato Shrozayemon, known as Toshiro, introducing stoneware about 1228 and Gerodayn Shonsui porcelain about 1513.

From this beginning the Japanese made rapid advances, and while, of course, for a time Chinese motifs were largely used, their natural artistic temperament soon asserted itself, and from being the scholar they came to be the masters of the Chinese, duplicating nearly all of their triumphs. Japanese pottery is primarily the expression of individuality, Chinese that of co-operative craftsmanship, for in Japan the whole working force of a pottery is often restricted to a single family, while Chinese pottery, on the contrary, represents the work of many, even the details of the painting being done by a number of artists.

The dominant religion of Japan is Buddhism, but with the exception of the seven gods of Good Fortune—Riches, Longevity, Daily Bread, Contentment, Learning, Military Glory and Love— depicted on their vases and reproduced in infinite variety as statuettes, it does not figure largely on their pottery. Their preference has been for domestic scenes when figures are employed, but their lakes and rivers, their trees and flowers, inspired those graceful and beautiful creations which are alike the envy and despair of the European potter. Their drawings of fish are wonderfully lifelike and alive, though as much cannot be said of the animals. The trees principally used are the fir, the bamboo and the plum, which together form an emblem of longevity. In flowers the favorite ones are the chrysanthemums, peonies, iris and water lily. From the prevalence of the first two named they have been given the distinction of a class "Chrysanthemopæonienne," and M. Jacquemart described them as Chinese, owing to their being marked with Chinese dates, although the date had passed away before porcelain was made in Japan. They are pre-eminent in their representation of birds, the crane, another emblem of longevity, being the most popular, though we find also eagles, hawks, pheasants, ducks, domestic fowl and a variety of small birds. Of monstrous animals there are the dragon, without the imperial signification of the Chinese, the tortoise, the kirin (the Chinese kylin) and the tortoise, the emblem of Japanese Imperial dignity. The badges of Japanese heraldry are also used as ornaments, including the chrysanthemum, the badge of the Emperor, the three leaves and flowers of the *Paulownia imperialis* of the Mikado and the three leaves and flowers of the mallow within a circle, of the Tycoon.

To understand Japanese shapes we must know something as to the purpose for which the articles were intended. The most important are the utensils for the tea ceremony, or cha-no-yu. Tea was introduced in Japan early in the thirteenth century, and soon afterwards the Shogun or Tycoon introduced these tea ceremonies. Rules for regulating them were made during the sixteenth century and the ceremonies improved. To-day they are simply friendly reunions. The articles used were a furnace for heating water; a water vase to hold water for washing the utensils; the tea jar; the tea bowl, and an ash pan. Simplicity was the keynote and the quality of the ware and glaze the indication of value.

Vessels for incense burning come next. They were of the most diverse character, sometimes taking the form of men, animals or birds. For keeping the hands warm a small earthenware brazier was used, somewhat pear shaped in form. For the writing table there were vases for holding and washing brushes, ink-stands and small vessels for water. These latter are of various forms, have a very diminutive spout to allow the water to escape drop by drop and a small hole on which to place the finger to regulate the flow. Teapots are of two forms, one like the European one, the other with a hollow handle at right angles with the spout. Cups are of the usual form, but without handles. Flower vases are of various forms. Plates were invariably saucer shape, those with flat rims being only made for export. Round and square bottles and jugs with spouts something like kettles are made for holding saké, which is usually drunk out of small cups sometimes graduated in size.

When we commenced to import Japanese ware, though we

acteristic Japanese features, which certainly cannot be said of the bulk of that received to-day, and nothing can be more incongruous than the imitations, not even skilfully done, of European styles now flooding the market, styles, too, which have in themselves nothing to commend them. This does not mean that the trade is restricted to these imitations, for many beautiful pieces can be found in the stores and at a comparatively small cost, examples of the best principles of decorative art and of potting.

INCENSE BURNER, SETO WARE. INCENSE BURNER, SATSUMA WARE

  In the case of Japan it seemed best for us to consider its pottery by provinces, the making of earthenware and porcelain being so closely associated as to make it difficult to trace the progress of each without going over the ground for a second time.

  In Owari the manufacture of stoneware by Toshiro was continued by his descendants for four generations, the ware being known as Ki-seto, ki meaning yellow from the color of the glaze. In 1801 Kato Tamikichi succeeded in making porcelain decorated in blue under the glaze, which is known as Sometsuki, the trade continuing to increase to the present day.

  Hizen may be considered the birthplace of Japanese glazed pottery. The Karatsu manufacturers revived the old Corean pottery, a painted variety being made in 1590. The manufacture declined about 1730. Modern Karatsu is a pale reddish brown stoneware with a crackle glaze. Arita is the most important seat of the industry and the products are generally known as Imari ware. Porcelain was first made here in 1503 by Ri-sampei, a

Corean, and its manufacture increased and in 1645 the exportation of what is known as "Old Japan" commenced. Tseiji Katsuzo is a distinguished manufacturer of the present day, his pierced pieces being triumphs of craftsmanship. Imari ware is familiar to us from its brilliancy of coloring, the disposition of painted panels of irregular shape on a ground of ornament and the lavish use of diapers. But perhaps most important were those pieces of white porcelain, with simple raised designs, the acme of artistic expression. It was pieces of this description that inspired Böttger, and its influence has affected the porcelain of all countries. The Koransha Company are celebrated manufacturers of to-day.

A KIOTO THROWER AT WORK.   WATCHING THE KILNS.

In the province of Idsumo is made the celebrated Raku ware, so much in favor for tea ceremonies. The word means "enjoyment."

Kioto.—Pottery was made at Awata as early as 1644-51 by a family named Nin Sei. The ware so called was of two kinds, an earthenware and a semi-porcelain. The former is now called Awata ware, and the latter, which has become a true porcelain, Kiyomidzu ware. Awata ware up to about 1873 was confined solely to light sketches of ceremonial opera performances in a few ои ведь by a broad gold outline. Later, designs of trees, birds, flowers and landscapes were used. The glaze is of a delicate yellow tint. To-day the potteries are mostly turning out wares for the American market and have lost their Japanese character. There is also produced a large quantity of imitation Satsuma. There are between twenty and thirty potteries in the Kioto district, the bulk of them with six or seven kilns ranged side by side. A good idea of these may be obtained from the illustration. Blue and white porcelain is also made and some very clever figures of poultry, etc. Among the potters who have made Kioto famous are the families of Dohachi for three generations and Rokubei, the fourth of that name, honorably maintaining their prestige at the present day.

Yeiraku ware is also made at Kioto. Originally the product consisted of earthenware braziers, but at the beginning of the nineteenth century Riosen commenced making porcelain, reproducing both old Japanese and old Chinese wares, especially the Chinese decoration consisting of coats of arms on a red ground. The Prince of Arita bestowed on him the title of Yeiraku, from which the ware takes its name. Some of the decorations resemble a rich brocade.

Island of Awaji.—The pottery here is a comparatively modern one (1840). The glaze is similar to that of Awata ware, is covered with a fine crackle and painted with enamels.

Satsuma Province.—We have already seen that this was of Corean origin. At first the manufacture consisted of a kind of stoneware glazed with lead and iron oxides. The finely crackled ware dates from about 1592, when the Prince of Satsuma brought several Corean potters home with him fom Corea. They settled first at Kagoshima, afterwards at Chiusa and eventually at Nawasherogawa, the seat of the manufacture of Satsuma ware. The ware with a gold outline was first made by a Corean named Koyo, about 1630. Colored decorations were not made much before the beginning of the nineteenth century. In addition to the distinctively Satsuma ware of a light buff with finely crackled glaze, there was also used a grayish white Corean clay, which was decorated by inlaying with it a white clay. This was reproduced at Ota, near Yokohama, by a potter named Kozan with such success that the original Satsuma ware lost its value. At the present day much of the pottery sold as Satsuma is made here.

Mizan of Satsuma to-day produces pieces of exquisite beauty and extreme delicacy of painting and finish.

Nawasherogawa is the only place in Japan in which a true Corean kiln exists. The kiln is built on the slope of a hill and is of peculiar construction, differing from that in Arita and other places. It is built singly and not in a line as in other factories. It has a length of one hundred and fifty to two hundred feet and a height of five feet in the center of a vault-like form. At the lower end of the kiln is a furnace, or, rather, the place to commence the firing. The fuel, consisting of dried wood, is thrown directly into the kiln, the inside of which communicates with the outer air by means of an opening in the side wall. Saggars are not used, and in consequence of this and the irregular distribution of heat throughout the kiln, great damage occurs to the ware.

The Corean potters number about 1,500, and since the establishment of the Central Government they enjoy the same rights and liberties as other subjects. Formerly they were not allowed to marry out of their own nationality.

Province of Kaga.—Kutani ware dates from the seventeenth century. Two clays are used, one a dark red of very uniform color found in the neighborhood, the other a dark gray. Red and gold in combination is a favorite coloring. A beautiful green was made here, which has recently been revived by Kechiji Watano, the same artist being very successful in his colored landscape designs after the famous Morikage style.

Miyagawa Kozan, before alluded to, although seventy years old, is to-day the first potter of Japan. His transmutation pieces with beautifully crystallized spots all over are triumphs of the potters' art. His copies of Chinese glazes are wonderful, and no less so are the carved pieces covered with a combination of celadon and white glazes.

Seifer, a pupil of Dohachi, whom he has excelled, continues to produce pottery of the finest description, his celadon glaze being unrivalled.

Kato Tomatora of Tokio is another present day potter of note, many of his works being enriched with a special shade of red known as Katoko.

Miura Chikusen, Kioto, famous for his blue and white, is also a literary man, and a few years ago published a book on Chinese Ceramics. In some of his pieces he introduces inlays of coral and stone. Kinkozan Sobei of Awata, Okumura Shozan and Kamamura Suzan of Kioto, Kechiji Watano of Kutani, Masatoro Keida of Satsuma are all eminent potters of to-day, the pierced and carved pieces of the latter being monuments of artistic skill and patient craftsmanship.

PERSIA.

If we try to chronologically follow the progress of the potters' art we must turn to Persia as being the legitimate successor to Egypt, Assyria and Babylon, even if to do so must be done through the Arabs, or Saracens, as they were called when they went to Europe to meet the Crusaders in Palestine. From these three countries Persia obtained her knowledge of processes, but her art was her own, and though modified by invaders it has always reasserted itself and retained its distinctive characteristics. Persia no less than China had the faculty of assimilating her conquerors and the same independence is notable in her art. Both Chinese and Saracenic influence was strongly felt, but were never allowed to be dominant.

When the Arabs overran Persia they were captivated by what they saw, and far from attempting to destroy they adapted it with such modifications as their religion allowed and as Saracenic ornament it was carried by them to Africa, Damascus and to Europe. In no place is there any record of their having introduced the making of pottery; what they did was to impress their superior art on what they found. Saracenic pottery then is no more than Persian modified by Arabian style. Among the earlier evidences of this are the tiles with which the domes and walls of mosques were covered, in which the influence of the new religion is apparent. Some of these have a metallic luster generally known as *reflets métalliques*. This process was certainly known to the Persians six or seven hundred years ago, and possibly two thousand, fragments having been found in the ruins of Rhages. It is interesting to note that this art became lost in Persia in the fourteenth century, it having in the meantime been carried into Spain by the Moors, where it again disappeared, only to reappear again in Italy in the seventeenth century, where it was finally lost, until the efforts of Ginori were rewarded by success late in the last century.

There was an early interchange of both workmen and pottery between China and Persia and one probably gave as much as the other. Many Chinese pieces undoubtedly show the influence of Persian art, even if not made by Persian workmen in China. A good example of this is the Aster pattern. The "Grains of Rice" porcelain has been by some writers identified with the Gombron ware of Horace Walpole, as being of Persian make, but both inferences are undoubtedly incorrect. All the known specimens are undeniably either Chinese or Japanese porcelain, and "Gombron," which for a long time puzzled ceramists as to its meaning, is a port on the Persian Gulf. It was acquired by the East India

Company in 1623, it being the port where for centuries the merchandise of China, India and Persia had been centralized. It was then the English custom to designate wares by the name of the port from which they were shipped, and in some instances Gombron seems to have been used in a generic sense, while in other cases a distinction is drawn between "Green Gombron" and "China," a word usd to designate blue and white painted ware. Anyway the term is a useless one and may well be allowed to be relegated to innocuous desuetude.

It has always been a disputed point as to whether true porcelain was ever made in Persia. A translucent ware was made, but the best authority we can find, Major R. Murdoch Smith, in

*PERSIAN TILES.

"Persian Art," is decidedly of opinion that it does not answer to the true definition of porcelain, inasmuch as it has not a vitreous break, but that the paste is, on the contrary, "porous or spongy and essentially earthenware." Chinese pottery was imitated, including the marks, and we know that in the seventeenth century Persian pottery was one of the principal articles exported to India and to Holland. Chardin relates that the Dutch sold this pottery to other European countries as Chinese, so that the manufacture must have been an important one in Persia at that time. It also helps to explain the presence of the numerous pieces of Chinese character found in that country.

Persian designs were excellent, ranging from intricate lace-like patterns to conventional flowers on which the rose and carnation predominated. On even the commonest pieces the utmost skill was lavished to render them veritable works of art. The articles made were nearly all pieces for use and consisted largely of bowls for sherbets dishes for rice, plates, water bottles, etc.

Imitations of Chinese celadon were made on a coarse body, for the Persian in his art, as in his daily life, thinks only of outside appearance, caring little for what is not seen. A general idea of the style will be obtained from the illustrations. Where a colored clay is used it is generally covered with a white flinty covering, very similar in appearance to a tin enamel. The coloring was extremely brilliant, the best colors being blue, turquoise, green and a peculiar red, like sealing wax, seen only on pieces made on the island of Rhodes, where the art was undoubtedly carried by Persian workmen. The art declined about the time of Shah Abbas II (1586-1628) and little of moment is made there now

RHODIAN PLACQUE.

SHRINE OF IMAN HUSSEIN AT KERBELA.
(Showing use of tiles.)

Tiles of large size dating from 1072 were made for ornamental tombstones and for embellishing the walls of mosques and other sacred buildings. As these are closed to Europeans, specimens are very rare, and what there are must have been obtained by stealth. Some of these have verses from the Koran, others inscriptions of a monumental character. Walls and floor tiles are still made at Teheran and other places.

The illustration showing the Holy Shrine at Kerbela is from a photograph in the South Kensington Museum, the only one in existence except those owned by the Shah.

CHAPTER VI.

JUSTA AND RUFINA. HISPANO-MORESQUE. NOBLE BUCCAROS. LUCCA DELLA ROBBIA. THE ITALIAN RENAISSANCE. GRAFFITO TIN ENAMEL IN GERMANY.

It is not possible to trace the progress of pottery in a direct line, for one may well assume that even when the art, made famous by some national exponent died, some remnant or tradition of it must have remained to blossom into newness of life in some unexpected place. But the important link which connected Europe with Persia and Africa is plainly visible. The Moors obtained their knowledge and largely adopted the style of the Saracenic potters. Where African pottery was made we have not much data, except that it flourished at Bagdad in the ninth century and at Cairo in the eleventh, contemporary writings stating that "there were then produced at Mise (Cairo) translucent vases of a hue which changed according to the positions given them," alluding no doubt to the *reflects métailliques* of the Persians. From Africa the art was carried to Spain. In this country, under the dominion of Rome, the Spaniards had acquired a certain proficiency in pottery and there is a curious legend handed down to us by the Roman Church of the time we mention, early in the fourth

JUSTA AND RUFINA.
From the painting by Goyo

century. At Seville there was a potter whose chief product seems to have been alcarazzas or water coolers. His two daughters, Justa and Rufina, had been converted to Christianity, the followers of which were much persecuted at the time. To be a Christian was just about equal to signing your death warrant. Being suspected, these two girls were ordered to provide alcarazzas for the shrine of Venus and to worship at the same. They steadfastly refused, strong in their newly found faith, were arrested and placed on the rack. As an additional incentive to their conversion to the old faith their sides were pierced with iron hooks. But they steadfastly refused to recant and won their martyrs' crown, Justa expiring on the rack, while Rufina's sufferings were ended by strangulation by order of the judge. Their bodies were then burned. Afterwards they were canonized by the church, and in Christian art the alcarazza became the emblem of the two patron saints of Seville. These water jars are now known in Spain as bucarro.

THE ALHAMBRA VASE.

The Arabs in their victorious march of conquest conquered Spain in the eighth century, and it is very remarkable that no specimens of pottery that can be definitely assigned to them are known. Five hundred years later, A. D. 1235, the Arabs were expelled by the Moors, the kingdom of Granada was formed and the Alhambra was built (1237). The Moors were not, however, left in undisputed possession, for James I of Aragon conquered Majorca in 1238 and extended his conquest the same year to the city of Valencia. In 1251 he granted a charter to the Moorish potters to continue their work there on payment of a small annual sum.

The Alhambra furnishes us with about the only examples of pottery of that period, the lavish tile work and the Alhambra vase. Upon their advent in Spain the Moors found a plentiful supply of tin and they abandoned the silicious covering they had previously used on their pottery and substituted a tin enamel.

The illustration will give a good idea of the Alhambra vase. The decoration is in a pure blue enamel on a white ground, with a gold luster over the whole. Three of these vases were found in a garden at the Adares, filled with treasure. Two of them were unfortunately broken and the pieces carried away by relic hunters, so means were then taken to preserve the remaining one. This vase was probably made about the middle of the fourteenth century. It has been reproduced at Sèvres, by Theodore Deck, and by Gomez of Triana, near Seville.

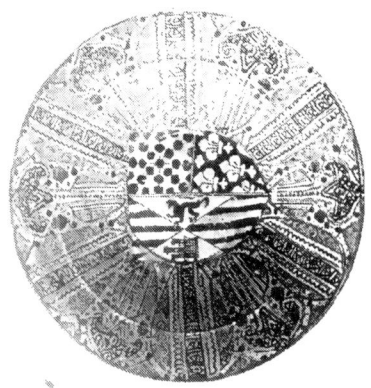

DISH WITH ARMS OF BLANCHE, QUEEN OF NAVARRE, VALENCIA (1419-1441).

The production of these lustered pieces by the Moors continued to progress, potteries were established at Malaga, Barcelona and Valentia. The latter progressed coincident with the deterioration of Malaga, while that of Barcelona was not important. The ware gradually lost its distinctive Moorish character, the lusters became more brilliant and consequently less pleasing, until they degenerated into a ruddy copper, and their lack of restraint marks the decline of Hispano-Moresque art. With the conquest of the Moors by Ferdinand and Isabella and their subsequent expulsion by Philip III, with the issuing of an edict in 1566 forbidding the use of Moorish ornament in decoration, came the collapse of the potters' art in Spain. This proved, if anything was needed, that it was entirely a foreign art and had no native characteristics.

We have not as yet alluded to the island of Majorca, usually thought to be the third great center of Hispano-Moresque pottery, and the place which is supposed to have given it its distinctive appellation, Majolica, or Maiolica. No pottery at all corresponding to what we are writing about was ever made there. Situated midway between Spain and Italy, it was the port from which the vessels that conducted the traffic between the two countries sailed.

So when the Italians received these specimens of pottery, brought to them on Majorcan vessels, they naturally thought them of Majorcan origin and may have been encouraged in this belief, for it was probably a profitable trade and the Majorcan would not be very anxious to acknowledge the source of supply. We have not space here to go thoroughly into the question, but those who are interested should read "Hispano-Moresque Ware of the XV Century," by A. van de Put, published by John Lane.

The distinctive Moorish character of this Hispano-Moresque ware gradually disappeared as it came more in contact with Christian art and in the fifteenth century, of which we have the most examples, it consisted of decorations of mock Arabic characters and borders and diapers of leaves, principally of the vine and briony. To this exception must be made to tiles or ajulejos, which retained their Moorish character, and some beautiful specimens of which adorn the Alhambra and the buildings of Seville and Granada. These tiles seem to be about the only articles of utility made by the Moors, the great bulk of the production being large dishes for purely ornamental purposes.

One searches in vain for evidences of a native art in Spain. It could have been dismissed in a paragraph had it not been that it was the stepping stone between Moorish art and the renaissance in Italy.

Simply on account of its geographical position, for it has never had any influence on ceramics, a passing mention of the buccaros of Portugal may be conveniently made here. During the sixteenth century the Portuguese imported from the heart of Central America large quantities of pottery, the clay of which was impregnated with a strong but delicate perfume, which communicated itself to any liquid placed therein and which became known as "Noble Buccaros." These were extremely diversified in shape and

DISH WITH ARMS OF MARY, CONSORT OF ALFONSO V. OF ARAGON.

many of them of such fantastic design as to have no parallel in existing pottery. The secret of their source was long kept by the Portuguese. They became the rage in Spain and Portugal and miraculous properties were invented for them. Small pieces were taken as a preventive of certain illnesses. Buccaro eating became the fashionable vice and there is recorded an instance of a lady eating a whole cup and saucer.

This scented pottery was reproduced in Portugal, the best being made at Lisbon, those of the manufacture Della Maya being most in request. Small pieces of buccaros, so costly had it become, were set by the jewelers in gold and silver and they commanded a large sale. But, after all, the perfume must have been evanescent, for though we have old pottery corresponding in every particular with the descriptions of old writers, not one solitary example of a Buccaro can we definitely recognize as such.

We have seen that the pottery credited to Majorca was in reality made in Spain and that the large number of pieces found in Italy are in reality Hispano-Moresque. It was nearly a hundred years from the time Malaga was in its zenith that Lucca della Robbia produced his first piece of white (A. D. 1440) or stanifferous enamel in Italy. This may have been an independent invention, though it is probable that the Spanish pottery was not unknown to him, or even some potter from Spain may have given him a hint. He was but about thirty-five years of age at the time, was a sculptor, not a potter, by profession, and if he discovered the glaze mixture, made a body on which it would fire evenly and fixed the point of firing to obtain such good results as his works show, it says much for his industry and perspicuity. Whether this is so or not is not material, but he is certainly to be credited with paving the way for those later triumphs in ceramics which culminated in the period from 1480 to 1530.

Lucca's bas-relief of "The Singing Boys" had brought him fame and with it a multiplicity of orders. Copies of his work by others did not keep pace with the demand, so he hit on the expedient of working in clay and the resultant discovery of tin enamel enabled him to produce as many copies as he wished. His first work in pottery was a bas-relief of the Resurrection, which can still be seen in the cathedral at Florence. In addition to his works in relief he also painted on the flat, twelve placques representing the months being good examples of this work. His modeled pieces are highly esteemed, being very beautiful both in design and execution and characterized by simplicity of treatment. The coloring was usually confined to blue and white, but occasionally a little green and yellow were used. At his death in 1481 he was succeeded by his nephew, Andrea, who at his death in 1528 was succeeded by his four sons. But neither the art of Andrea or his four sons was equal to that of Lucca. The style passed away in the early part of the sixteenth century. Nearly all of Lucca della Robbia's works have been reproduced of late years and many of them are excellent.

Already some strides had been made in Italy prior to Robbia's invention. Castel-Durante is on record as making pottery in 1361, though there are no known examples: Pesaro in 1450, and Faenza prior to 1475, there being a Faenza dish in the Musée de Cluny bearing that date, six years before Lucca della Robbia died. It was a time when men's souls were awakening from the oblivion of centuries, the tide of the renaissance was beginning to flow, the some time neglected enamel was remembered, and many artists saw in it imperishability for their work and seized on it with avidity. The great reigning princes of Urbino (the birthplace of Raphael), of Pesaro and Florence, the Montefeltros, the Sforza, the Medici and the Fontanos united in extending to it their patronage. A successful potter was created a Maestro, he was the social equal of princes. There were half a dozen or more centers where the art flourished, each as great as the other. They came into existence a few years apart, from 1477 to 1524; they reached their zenith but a few years later, a decline in the art being noticeable after 1560. There is a strong family likeness in this Italian painted pottery and it has been found difficult to assign dates and locality to many pieces which have no marks But few articles of utility were made, most of them being entirely for decorative purposes and the adornment of houses and palaces. The greatest artists of the times made designs for this pottery, including the great Raphael. An exception to this is the pharmacy jars, of which large numbers were made. They are usually divided in four sections, painted mostly in yellow on a blue

PAINTED PLACQUE, 22½ INCHES IN DIAMETER, BY LUCCA DELLA ROBBIA.

ground, a head or medallion on one side, under which is the name of the drug in gothic lettering on a ribbon.

There were no large manufactories as we understand such to-day. A man embarked in the pottery trade, established his botega—a compromise between a factory and a studio—and employed the best artists he could to do the painting, without his being permanently attached to the staff. Other botegas were attached to the courts and castles of princes and nobles, producing work only for their patrons. Again, artists purchased the ware, decorated it and disposed of it as they could.

At first the range of colors was very limited and many of the pieces have a sickly appearance, yellow being used for flesh tints. Originally the colors were painted on the unfired enamel, a process which necessitated quick manipulation, and as both enamel and color were fired at the same time, very soft and harmonious results were obtained.

We have spoken of the princely patronage accorded to the italian potters who, by their financial aid and appreciation, did so much in the cause of art. Let us see what part it played in the Duchy of Urbino, which embraced Pesaro, Castle-Durant, Urbino and Gubbio. At Pesaro, according to Passeri, who was born there and to whom we are indebted for much information about Italian pottery, Majolica was made there as early as 1462. In 1486 and 1508 the Sforza family interested themselves in the pottery, for in those years edicts were passed against the importation of earthenware into Pesaro. These measures were commemorated by a placque with portraits of Giovanni Sforza and his mother, Camilla, with a scroll representing the edict as a background. The decoration is in blue, enriched with ruby and gold lusters. But it was Duke Guidobaldo II who came to the Duchy of Urbino in 1538, who raised it to the rank it afterwards attained. It was Pesaro that first produced pottery with portraits and amatory devices (amatorii) which possess so much value as records of costumes of the day. At Urbino this same duke raised the art from comparative insignificance to the very front rank, its productions being considered the most artistic and most remarkable product of the sixteenth century. They were considered fit presents to send to foreign potentates. Three celebrated artists contributed much to its success, Guido Fontano, his son, Orazio, and Francisco Xanto Avelli da Rovigo, known as Xanto. Guido Fontano was the first to cover the whole of the piece with decoration without regard to its form, a fault somewhat redeemed by his brilliant coloring and faultless execution. Xanto's productions were mostly in the nature of compositions arranged from

A POTTERY PRIMER. 49

engravings after Raphael. There is a great diversity of opinion as to his ability as an artist, some critics defending, others condemning him for his monotonous and mechanical work. The best known work of Urbino is the series of 380 vases, etc., made by order of Guidobaldo II and now in the Santa Casa of Loretto. Louis XIV offered for the figures of the four evangelists and St. Paul an equal number of statues in gold. These magnificent vases were mostly painted by the Fontano family, though other well known artists were employed. The remainder of the duke's collection passed to the Medici and is now in the museum at Florence.

CASTEL-DURANTE PLACQUE.   GUBBIO PLACQUE (About 1518).

Gubbio, too, was under ducal patronage and Giorgio Andreoli, better known as Maestro Giorgio, has rendered it immortal. He was not only a painter, but a sculptor, and executed considerable work in the style of Lucca della Robbia. His work consisted of foliated scrolls and other ornaments terminating in dolphins, eagles, etc., showing much skill and inventive power, enclosing figure subjects, coats of arms, etc. His lusters were unapproachable and it shows much for his devotion to his art that he consented to enrich the works of his contemporaries by the application of his inimitable lusters. The title of Maestro was coveted made precious and not lightly bestowed.
and esteemed as highly as nobility, it was a Legion of Honor
Castel-Durant is a small town near Urbino. Among its products were pharmacy jars, decorated with grotesques on a black ground. Its other products are similar to that of Urbino.

There were many other potteries in Italy besides those mentioned, and the imitation of the art is variously ascribed to Caffaggiola, Faenza and Pesaro. There are dated pieces of Caffaggiola, which was under the patronage of the Medici, of 1507 and 1509. The glaze is of a very rich and even quality and the blue as brilliant as lapis lazuli.

Faenza had several potteries, one of which was the Casa Pirota. Its works were of the highest quality, admirable alike in design and execution. Borders of grotesques in blue on a white ground, enclosing central designs, predominated and the works of three clever artists are traceable, though their names are unknown. Later, that is the sixteenth century, when painting covered the whole of the surface, Faenza ware is difficult to distinguish from other Italian pieces. On Faenza, Urbino and other wares may be seen the initials S. P. Q. F., meaning the Senate and people of Florence. There were also potteries at Forli, Rimini, Ravena, Siena, Ferrara, Deruta and perhaps Florence.

With the end of the sixteenth century the Italian ware ceased to have artistic merit, the special features that had characterized it were abandoned and it was allowed to sink into oblivion.

Before passing on to trace the progress of tin enamel we must allude to the incised ware of the Italians, variously called Sgraffiati, Sgraffiato and Graffito. The process had been used from primitive times and consists of covering the ware with a slip of another color which is then scratched through with a tool to show the body underneath, thus forming the pattern. It was extensively employed by the Italians of the twelfth and thirteenth centuries who dignified it into an art.

Let it be noted that in cases where the pottery was not covered with a tin enamel, but with a white slip on which the subject was painted and then covered with a lead glaze and afterwards lustered, it was distinguished by the name "Mezza-Majolica."

In Germany the tin enamel appears to have been known earlier than in Italy, the Germans ascribing it to an Alsatian potter who died in 1283. It was known to Hirschvogel of Nuremburg and specimens dating from 1470 by him are known. The vase illustrated is 20 inches high and is decorated with scenes from the life of Christ, notably the Crucifixion. It was sold a year or so ago for $900. But it is to France rather than Germany we must look

HIRSCHVOGEL VASE.

for a perpetuation of this stanifferous pottery

CHAPTER VII.

DELFT. FAIENCE D'OIRON. BERNARD PALISSY. NEVERS. ROUEN. MOUSTIERS. ENGLISH DELFT.

By this time Oriental pottery was being imported into Europe and the potters of that continent were searching for the materials which would enable them to produce it. The trend of these experiments, the superstitious beliefs as to the composition of the body and the results achieved will be told elsewhere. Early in the seventeenth century the Dutch, who were then the leading traders, had established a large trade with the Orient, and this Oriental pottery stimulated the Dutch to attempt something similar in character. The movement centered in the town of Delft, which had no pottery traditions, its industries having been mainly confined to beer and wool. At one time nearly three hundred breweries lined its canals.

We are told that as early as 1310 there are examples, or rather records, of pottery in Delft, but if this is so the industry became extinct, for according to M. Havard, the authority on Delft pottery, the archives of the town are silent on that point up to the seventeenth century, and this is emphasized by the fact that in 1596 a list is given of the trades permitted in the town, in which pottery is not included.

The selection of a town like Delft for a pottery center, with no natural resources, suggests the inquiry as to why it was selected. We think the answer is that it was to provide an industry to replace one or more lost ones. From 1573 to 1584 Delft had been the residence of William the Silent, and the presence of the court had made it to some extent an artistic center—William's successor, Maurice, never resided in Delft, and in consequence the town lost much of its social and artistic character and was deserted by the tapestry workers, goldsmiths, etc. The manufacture of cloth seemed to have died out and the breweries were beginning to decline. It was probably Herman Pieterz who inaugurated the idea of pottery. The potters were formed into a guild called the Guild of St. Luke, which is first mentioned in 1611. Two years later (1613) was commenced the "Masters' Books" of the guild, eight master potters being inscribed therein, the first on the list being Herman Pieterz, another was Thomas Janz (Thomas Jones), an Englishman. This guild grew mightily; an examination had to be passed by every member and it eventually contained no less than 763 ceramists. Many of the potteries had distinguishing signs, such as "The Claw," "Three Bells," the "Porcelain Hatchet," the "Porcelain Bottle," etc. As we have said, Delft had no natural advantages for the manufacture of pottery, the clay being obtained from Tournai and the Rhine. There are three periods of Delft pottery, the first from its inception up to 1650, characterized by an extremely full decoration usually in blue, the subjects represented being mostly historical and battle scenes containing a great number of figures. The ground was a white enamel which gained in brilliancy by the hard fire it was capable of receiving without impairing the quality of the blue. This was covered with a transparent lead glaze, applied by shaking the glaze on the enamel with a brush, both being fired at the same time. This had the effect of heightening the color.

In the second period, 1650-1710, the art lost something of its distinctive and national characteristics, but is remarkable for its reproductions of Oriental wares, not only in blue but also in reds, greens, yellow and gold. Three well known potters of this period were Pynacker, Fictoor and Van Eenhorn, who made beautiful polychrome decorations on a blue ground. The blue and whites wares were also considerably improved and while the subjects were often Chinese, many Dutch landscapes and rural scenes were also made. The third period extended from 1710 to its decline, and the productions were purely commercial, not that no artistic goods were produced for such was far from the case. The grotesques of the Japanese were reproduced and imitated and this led to exaggerated forms which possessed neither the humor of the Japanese nor their originality and were displayed in such abortions as vegetable dishes in the form of birds, etc. These and similar things may be curious, they are certainly not artistic, for only can an utilitarian article be so classed when it is best adapted to the purpose for which it is intended and the lines of it are as simple as possible.

There is a story of a Delft potter, who is said to have made four fäience violins on the occasion of the wedding on the same day of his four sons. Champfleury, a French writer, took this as a motive, and from it evolved his charming "A Fäience Violin," the most dependable work of fiction in which pottery figures, that we know of.

With the extinction of the simplicity that first characterized Delft pottery and the competition of English earthenware the industry gradually declined and finally decayed towards the end of the eighteenth century.

Before tracing the progress of tin enameled ware to the Normandy potters, we must note the production in France of two isolated examples of the potters art. The one is the pottery of Bernard Palissy, the other Fäience d' Oiron, also known under the names of Henri Deux and Saint Porchaire ware. There now seems no reason to doubt that it was made at the Château d' Oiron near Thouars, from 1524 to 1537, under the direction of the widow of Arthur Gouffier, Hélène de Hengest, a woman of refined and artistic taste. In collaboration with her were two skilful and intelligent men, Jehan Bernart, her librarian, and François Charpentier, to whom she deeded in 1529 the house and orchard where the pottery was made. Hélène de Hengest died in 1537, and the pottery was continued under the patronage of her son Claude Gouffier until about 1568, when it fell into the hands of inexperienced men and rapidly declined. There is a particular charm about this pottery when we remember that at that period nothing but the most ordinary wares were made in France, when Italy was committed to the tin enamel before the rise of Delft, and Germany had practically little more than the Nuremberg pottery, and it is certainly remarkable that this distinct type should be created in this obscure place with no pottery traditions. It is the more remarkable as apart from the exquisite quality of the workmanship, it presented technical difficulties of no mean order, difficulties which, as far as we know, have been surmounted in modern times by but one craftsman, Charles Toft, who successfully duplicated some of these pieces for Minton of Stoke-upon-Trent. It was by no means a commercial venture, the pieces being evidently made for presentation. At first the forms were extremely simple, but as the potters grew accustomed to their material, enrichments were added, the forms lost their simplicity and became very ornate. But on all the utmost pains and most loving care was bestowed on the decorative enrichments. The body is a fine white clay, and on this the pattern was impressed or incised and the sunk portion was filled up with different colored clays, yellow, buff and brown. There could not have been the same shrinkage during the drying and firing in all these clays, and the adjustment of these in the perfectly marvelous manner in which it was accomplished, gives them their chief value. The patterns of an intricate nature are more easily accounted for and were no doubt suggested by the ornate book bindings by Groller and others of that period. Introduced in the designs the cypher of Henri II. is found on several pieces, and this gave rise to the name Henrideux ware. Of this ware there are but fifty-three known examples, and they are valued at $140,000, but would undoubtedly bring much more if sold to-day. They may be regarded as one of the curiosities of the ceramic art, a triumph of technical skill, an everlasting monument to the genius of their creator.

The indomitable perseverance of the French potter, Bernard Palissy, soon afterwards added another ceramic triumph to the credit of France. Born about 1510, he married in 1539, and took up his abode at Saintes. He seems to have practiced both glass painting and surveying. A cup of enameled earthenware which some way came under his observation, inspired him with the desire to imitate it. He has himself written the story of his life, his hopes and aspirations, his disappointments and the dire stress of poverty, but no word does he tell us of the secret of his glaze. It was a strange and marvelous quest, "a grouping in the dark," as he himself writes, and became an obsession. Failure followed failure, brightened now and then by gleams of encouragement which only lured him on to new experiments, to poverty one degree greater than before. In the open graves of his children he looked sorrowfully down, in the emaciated faces of those who still lived, and in that of his wife he read his condemnation, but he never swerved. The idea had got hold of him and held him, and enthusiast, madman—call him what you like—he stopped at nothing. Without money, his credit absolutely exhausted there came the time when to feed the kiln, the doors and window frames of his house were used as fuel, yet still the glaze had not melted. In a moment of courage or madness, taunted and reviled by his neighbors, the few scanty pieces of furniture he owned, went into the kiln's insatiable maw, and the glaze dissolved, the result for which he had given sixteen years of his life had been attained.

FAIENCE D' OIRON BIBERON.

It would be well perhaps to modify this statement, for although we do not know what the original cup was that inspired Palissy, it was reasonable to suppose that it was as he says, "enameled," and possibly may have been made at Nuremberg, or was one of the opaque enamels of Limoges. If this is so he must have abandoned his original idea for what he produced was a transparent colored glaze of various colors.

The best know of his works are his *pièces rustiques*, which are ornamented with fish, frogs, snakes, shells, leaves and other natural objects, and are covered with colored transparent glazes. These objects were first arranged in the desired form, and by pouring plaster over them a mold was obtained. Much cannot be said for their artistic value, but their technical excellence is unquestionable, especially when we consider the common materials from which they were evolved. In addition to these he

*PALISSY DISH.

utilized the beautiful creations of François Briot, using his ewers and plates from which to make molds, and later must have employed artists of renown to model his more original figure subjects.

He became a convert to the teachings of the Reformation, was arrested in 1558 and imprisoned at Bordeaux, his kilns and workshops being destroyed. He was liberated in 1563 and set up a pottery in Paris where he lived and prospered until 1588, when he was thrown into the Bastile, and refusing his liberty at the price of recantation (fancy Palissy recanting) he was condemned to death, but died in 1589, before sentence was carried out. It was in the Bastile that he wrote the story of his life,

*PALISSY DISH AFTER BRIOT.

rich in philosophical and religious meditations, but almost devoid of particulars as to his pottery. The French profess to regard this work as one of exceptional merit, Lamartine seeing there the grace of Montaigne, the graphicness of Rousseau and the poetry of Bossuet.

*PALISSY JARDINIERE.

An attempt was made to continue Pallisy's work, but for want of knowledge of the processes it was soon abandoned as a failure.

Frequent attempts have been made to reproduce Palissy pieces, some clumsy imitations, others of considerable merit, but the best are by Avisseau, of Tours, whose work is so like the original as to deceive the most expert. Palissy pieces being of great value, his temperance dish (a copy of a pewter) selling in 1886 for over five thousand dollars, Avisseau was approached by certain dealers to issue his copies unsigned, but to his own credit and that of humanity, he refused, and all pieces made by him bear his name. These in turn will become valuable just as have the pieces of Fäience d' Oiron made by Toft.

There were several attempts made to introduce the tin enamel in France which did not prove successful. One of these was at Lyons about the middle of the sixteenth century and another one at Nantes, both founded by Italian potters.

Girolamo della Robbia, a grandson of Lucca della Robbia, in the time of Francis I was entrusted with the decoration of part of the *Petit chateau de Madrid*,

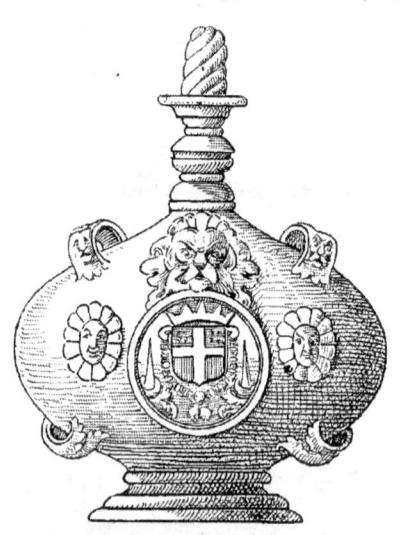

PALISSY HUNTING FLASK WITH ARMS OF MONTMORENCY.

or, as it was nicknamed, *Chateau de fäience,* because the outside walls were covered with pottery and enamels. It was destroyed by fire in 1792, and, unfortunately, no effort was made to preserve specimens of the pottery used in its construction. It is surmised that Masseot (Thomas) Abaquesne, of Rouen, who is known through documentary evidence only, may have worked for Girolamo, and so learned the secret of the enamel.

This documentary evidence about pottery of which there are no known examples sometimes receives startling confirmation Jean de Valence, a Saracen, was known to have worked at P tiers from 1383 to 1387, but it was not until 1904 that M. Lucien Magne discovered undoubted examples of his work with staniferous enamel and *réflets métalliques*. The same gentleman, in his explorations at the Château de Saumar, has found other evidences of the manufacture of tiles essentially differing from the foregoing, which may help to elucidate several doubtful points, but at this moment M. Magne has not communicated to the world their exact nature, nor are his explorations in the Château by any means complete.

For some reason the potteries we have mentioned only existed a short time, and the real history of the tin enamel centers in the Normandy potteries, of which Nevers was the earliest and Rouen the most celebrated. Nor did these potteries spring from the initiative of the French potter. The Duke of Nivernais about the middle of the sixteenth century brought to France a number of Italian artists and craftsmen, among whom was a potter named Scipion Gambin, of Faenza, who settled at Nevers. He produced ware in the style of Faenza and Urbina, and the former being his native town it is easy to see how the products would be alluded to, perhaps at first, as "in the style of Faenza," later as simply "Faenza ware," until the word began to have a generic character and was softened into faïence. His wares lacked one characteristic of the Italian, inasmuch as a transparent glaze was not added to the white enamel. The subjects were mostly mythological or historical subjects, the outlines traced in brown. The manufacture was not very important and, we think, might easily have decayed, like those of Lyons and Nantes, but for the advent of the brothers Conrade, Italians from Savona, who in 1608 had a manufactory at Nevers. In place of the polychrome decoration they reverted to the simpler blue, discarded the figure subjects in favor of ornament, though this was often injudiciously arranged, various styles, such as Chinese and Italian, being mixed together. The Conrades for three generations successfully carried on the business. But the greatest ceramic claim Nevers possesses is in the beautiful pieces with a dark blue ground decorated with white enamel, of so much excellence as for a long time to deceive experts as to their origin, the learned Brongniart ascribing them to Persia. Pierre Custode was contemporary with the Conrades and had a pottery there in 1632, known as l'Autruche (the Ostrich). About the end of the seventeenth and beginning of the eighteenth centuries Chinese influence asserted itself and gave a certain character to the productions, but the Chinese designs were often inappropriately used and often mixed with Italian motifs. Then came the coarsely painted ware, with figures of saints and the name of the person for whom they were intended, which quickly degenerated as the Italian influence waned. These were followed by heavy and common ware, in which the so-called "Fäiences Patriotiques" must be included, which were covered with unsightly daubs, and beyond which badness could hardly go.

Some of the Nevers potters must have migrated to Rouen, for from about 1644 to 1673 we find pottery showing Italian influence. About the latter date there was introduced by Louis Poterat a style of decoration so distinct that it is always identified as Rouenaise, and is essentially French. The most popular decoration was termed *à lambrequins*, which consists of two alternate corresponding designs repeated so as to form a border. The lambrequins were composed of leaves, scrolls, etc., in white on a blue ground, and sometimes heightened with Indian red, a color not used at Nevers. The disposition of the ornament is always symmetrical and, contrary to what we should imagine at first glance, of extreme simplicity. These designs were largely adapted from textile fabrics, lace, the tail pieces to be found in books of the period, etc. An elaboration of these designs was termed *style rayonnant*, in which similar patterns radiated from the center. Afterwards these pattern were made in a variety of colors and Chinese designs were used, and a potter named Guillibaud introduced a border of black and red check alternating with white spaces on which were sprays of flowers. Soon afterwards the cornucopia pattern was introduced and, from the number of specimens, must have been very popular. Single and double cornucopias from which flowed a shower of flowers, birds, insects, etc., painted in brilliant colors, red and yellow predominating. There was a great variety of articles made, both for useful and ornamental purposes, and among the latter large busts and pedestals, the best of these by Nicholas Fouquay (1740), who succeeded Poterat. Other pieces were wall fountains, helmet ewers, church lamps, brackets, spice boxes, etc. How extensive was the production may be judged from the fact that early in the eighteenth century over two thousand people were engaged in the industry. The proverb that it is an ill wind that blows no one any good is well exemplified by the Rouen potteries. At the time we speak of the finances of France were about exhausted by the con-

NEVERS VASE.

NORMANDY POTTERY.

tinuous wars, much misery had been caused by the inundation of the Loire and there was a disastrous famine in 1709. The King

ROUEN DISH á *Lambrequins.*  SCHOOL OF ROUEN.

and court sent all objects of gold that they possessed to the mint to be coined, and substituted faience for the gold plate they had used. This gave a great impetus to the pottery trade in Rouen and the manufacturers vied with each other to produce objects of art. With the growth of the porcelain industry and the treaty of commerce with England admitting Staffordshire pottery, the manufacture of faience in Rouen came to a close.

But it was a great ceramic achievement; the skill displayed

MOUSTIERS DISH.  SCHOOL OF MOUSTIERS.

A POTTERY PRIMER.

had been remarkable, and it is to-day an object lesson as to the suitability of the design to the shape it was to decorate.

The success of Rouen led to the establishment of many potteries elsewhere, but we can only give them a passing notice. Most of them commenced with servile imitations of Rouen, and later developed into more original styles. The Parisian potters excelled in the manufacture of chimney pieces and stoves, some of the former being works of art in all sense of the term. St. Cloud, later to become famous for soft porcelain, commenced with the manufacture of faience. Sincenny, founded by Pierre Pillive, a Rouen man, made faience equal to that of Rouen, and both at Lille and Quimper good ware was made. Moustiers did not slavishly copy Rouen, but originated styles distinctively its

STRASBURG FOUNTAIN. SCHOOL OF STRASBURG.

own. One of these consisted of wreaths of flowers and small medallions, softly and harmoniously painted. The enamel was also very pure. Copies of the fine engravings of the celebrated Florentine, Antonio Tempesta, the subjects being hunting or battle scenes, were successfully painted on large plaques. Eventually Moustiers founded a school, just as Rouen had done. Of these may be mentioned Varages, Taverne, Marseilles, Quimper and Clermont-Ferrand.

There was still a fourth distinctive pottery center in addition to Nevers, Rouen and Moustiers, Strasburg, founded in 1709 by Charles Hannong and continued by his sons and grandsons until about the end of the century. Porcelain was successfully made, but in 1750 this was stopped by order of the King the kilns destroyed, so that the protected business at Vincennes might not be interfered with, a very effective way of stifling competition. The Hannongs then turned their attention again to faience, employing the processes used for decorating porcelain, thus creating a new type. The shapes were of greater elegance, the decorations, mostly detached flowers, were executed with great dexterity and the enamel was of a milky whiteness. Many large decorative faience pieces were produced, clocks, fountains, etc., beautifully modeled and painted, and dishes with pierced borders were for the first time made in France. So great was the success of the Strasburg faience that it was taxed much more heavily than similar wares, the tariff on foreign goods being applied to it and it being impossible to continue its manufacture under such conditions the industry came to an end. Of the school of Strasburg were Niedeviller, founded about 1742, celebrated for the artistic supervision of Madame de Beyerlé and the sculptures of Charles Sauvage, generally called Lemire, and Lunéville, to whose success the charming statuettes of Cyffle largely contributed. Nancy, founded in 1774, made statuettes by Clodeon, so highly esteemed that they are now worth their weight in gold. Apt, under the direction of the widow Arnoux, has a claim on our consideration, inasmuch as the widow Arnoux was the grandmother of Leon Arnoux, to whose genius much of the success of the celebrated Minton factory is due. We can but catalog the remaining French potteries, Islettes, from 1737 to 1830; Aprey, Marseilles, Sceaux, Rennes, Bordeaux, Montpellier, St. Amond-les Eaux and Orléans. The three illustrations from Garnier's "Dictonnaire de la Céramique," showing the styles that dominated the schools of Rouen, Moustiers and Strasburg are worthy of special study.

In England the tin enamel or delft ware, as it was called, never took permanent root. Dutch potters established several potteries in Lambeth early in the seventeenth century. From there it drifted to other centers, Bristol, Liverpool and Staffordshire. Of these the Lambeth was the best, but is easily distinguished from the Dutch, as the latter was entirely covered with the enamel, while the surface only of the former was covered, the back being finished with a lead glaze. Some of the Liverpool tiles are worthy of notice, especially the engraved designs of Carver, made by Sadler & Green, printed by the process invented by J. Sadler. Liverpool delft is usually distinguished by its bluish tint, while that of Bristol inclines more to green and the Lambeth to a faint rose.

The large dishes with so-called portraits of William and

Mary, the Duke of Marlborough and other personages of the time, and known as "Blue Chargers," were possibly made at several of the named localities. They vary so much in character as to prohibit the idea that one locality was responsible for them. Some are well conceived and fairly well executed, while others are mere daubs impossible to tolerate. The locality where this English delft ware was made in Staffordshire is still known as Lane Delft.

The rapid improvement made in Staffordshire earthenware made it impossible to continue the production of delft. The clay was not suitable to the enamel, being much denser than that of delft, and this caused the enamel to craze. It was perhaps the one form of pottery from a foreign source the English potter failed to improve, and as it was by no means equal to the local product its manufacture was abandoned.

CHAPTER VIII.

GRES DE FLANDRES—JOHN DWIGHT.

The introduction of stoneware in Europe is generally conceded to Germany, though there is a curious story of Jacquelaine of Bavaria, Countess of Hainault and Holland, considerably antedating the earliest known German example, a fragment of brown Raeren ware dated 1539. She appears to have been the storm center of troublous times, at one time leading an army in company with her lover, the Duke of Gloucester, against her husband, twice imprisoned and finally forced to cede her possessions to Philip "the Good" (save the mark) and retire to the privacy of the castle of Teylingen. Here she occupied herself with the superintendence of a pottery, and is said to have worked in it herself. After her death in 1436, at the age of thirty-six, the small jugs made there were thrown into the moat "that they might in after ages be deemed works of antiquity." None of those discovered is of any artistic merit. They are generally known as "Vrou Jacoba's Kannetjes."

It is to Germany in the sixteenth century that we are indebted for the salt-glazed stoneware, generally known as "Grès de Flandres." This was a distinct departure from anything before known in ceramics, the creation of a type. As such it calls for a few words of explanation. The body was hard and impervious, granular in texture and distinctly suggestive of its name—stoneware. The clays used were a creamy white, a rich brown and a slaty gray. The pieces were thrown on the whee and then enriched with various patterns made from molds and fastened to the surface by means of slip, exactly the same as the Wedgwood jasperware was made. So far it lacked its chief characteristic, the glaze. Previously this had been applied in a powder on the ware, but the stoneware glaze was formed by throwing common sea salt into the kiln when the heat was highest, which vaporized and united with the clay, forming a beautiful granulated glaze similar to the skin of an orange. Many attempts have been made to account for the discovery of salt glazing, none bear investigation, and the credit of it must be ceded to these German potters. Owing to the nature of the body, which was liable to crack with heat or hot water, the manufacture was mostly confined to beer jugs, tankards and ornamental pieces. From Germany the making of stoneware passed to Holland and from there to England. Before taking up the story there, a few words as to its generic title "Grès de Flandres," is

FULHAM STONEWARE.   HOUND HANDLED TYG.

in order. Flanders at that time embraced part of Holland, Belgium and France, and all the "Low Countries" were known to outsiders as Flanders. Raeren, before alluded to, one of the seats of manufacture, was in Limbourg. The ports of shipment were Flemish ports, and as in many other instances, the ware was so designated, the slatey gray clay suggesting the prefix.

There were several attempts made in England to introduce the manufacture of stoneware, but all traces of the productions have been lost, until we come to the time of **John Dwight**, of Fulham, the first important name on the rôle of honor of English pottery. Dwight, like Böttcher, Palissy and others, was not a potter by trade, but was evidently lured into the business by the desire of discovering the secret of Oriental china. While he did not accomplish this, he succeeded in producing stoneware of the ...... in the words of M. Solon, "To him must be attributed the foundation of an important industry by his unremitting researches and their practical application, he not only found the means of supplying in large quantities the daily wants of the people with an article superior to anything that had ever been known before, but besides, by the exercise of his refined taste and uncommon skill, he raised the craft to a high level; nothing among the masterpieces of ceramic art of all other countries can excel the beauty of Dwight's brown stoneware figures, either for design, modeling or fineness of material."

The manufactory at Fulham was established in 1671, and in addition to the figures alluded to by M. Solon large quantities of jugs, mugs, etc., were made. Many of the former were in the shape of Bellarmines or Graybeards, having the grotesque head impressed on the neck; others with crests and badges, or figures of birds and animals, probably having reference to the inns for which they were intended. The manufacture of these by Dwight's descendants was continued long after his death. From Fulham the manufacture of brown stoneware spread to Nottingham, Chesterfield and Derby, the ornamentation instead of being in relief, being incised in the clay.

It is to these localities we owe the black bear jugs, and jugs and mugs with handles in the shape of a greyhound, all of which seem to have been extremely popular.

In continuation of this subject the work of the Elers Brothers and the creation in England of a new type of salt glazed stoneware would be in logical sequence, but as it forms such an important part in the history of English ceramics we will defer its consideration, so as not to go over the ground twice, until we deal with the pottery of that country.

To-day England and Germany share the honors in the production of stoneware, the creations of the Lambeth Doulton and the Villeroy & Boch Mettlach ware being equally meritorious.

CHAPTER IX.

PORCELAIN IN EUROPE—ARTIFICIAL PORCELAIN.

When Oriental porcelain first became known in Europe it was regarded with an almost superstitious veneration, and many wonderful theories were advanced as to its manufacture. The Chinese kept the composition of the paste as a great secret and evidently tried to lead inquirers astray by all kinds of fantastic stories. Barbosa, a celebrated Italian physician (died 1576), and his contemporaries, Jerome Cardan, Scaliger and Panciroti, the learned antiquary of Padua, describe the body as being composed of the shell of marine locusts, bruised eggs, gypsum and other ingredients, which had to be buried underground for eighty to a hundred years before being ready to use. This story was probably the basis for Dr. Johnson's fanciful derivation of the word porcelain—*pour cent annes*. It was further said that vases made of this paste had the wonderful property that if poison was put in them they immediately burst asunder; that he who buried the matter never saw it again, but left it as a legacy to his heirs, being much more valuable than gold. The secret, however, leaked out, but as no kaolin was known to exist in Europe, men set to work to discover a substitute. This resulted in the production of soft porcelain, or, as it was later called at Sèvres, *pate tendre*. Let us note here that a soft porcelain is an artificial combination of various materials, agglomerated by the action of fire in which a frit has been used as a substitute for the natural rock. A frit is a mixture of sand and alkali, fused together in the fire, then ground up and mixed with clay and other ingredients to form the paste. This soft porcelain was made in Venice as early as 1504-1519, and at Vienna in 1575 but no specimens are known. The earliest known example is the Medici porcelain made at Florence in 1580, under the patronage of the Medici family. The decorations were chiefly in blue under the glaze; the paste was heavy and not very white. There are but about thirty known specimens of this ware. Japanese influence is plainly discernable.

The Capo di Monte works were founded in 1736 by Charles III, but notwithstanding his connection by marriage with the court of Saxony the china produced at Capo di Monte had nothing in common with that of Meissen, being a soft or artificial body. The first attempts were inspired by Japanese pottery, but very quickly assumed a distinctive character. The Bay of Naples furnished the *motifs*, and seashells, seaweed and coral were ingeniously combined in the construction of some of their most beautiful work. These were colored naturally, and the coral red used for handles, etc., is a characteristic feature. A ewer formed of an ingenious combination of shells, set in a foot of coral, a branch of which climbs up the sides and, arching outward, forms the handle, will illustrate the style. Figures of cupids, sea nymphs, etc., were introduced in the designs, and the flesh parts of these were always most carefully painted—not in washes, but by careful and laborious stippling. The table services made at Capo di Monte were splendid examples of potting, the paste being fine and transparent and almost as delicate as the Chinese eggshell. Beautiful *bas-reliefs*, statuettes, etc., in white bisque were also produced. The King is stated to have personally worked in the pottery in addition to attending to its finances. When he was called to the throne of Spain in 1759 he determined to take his china works with him.

Prince Ferdinand removed what was left to Portici and afterwards to Naples, but the guiding spirit had passed away and the works were closed in 1821. Some of the molds came into the hands of Ginori, who has continued to reproduce them.

REPRODUCTIONS OF CAPO DI MONTI BY GINORI.

At Buen Ritrio the whole product was reserved for imperial use until after the death of Charles in 1788, the traditions of Capo di Monte being closely followed. Later reproductions of Sèvres and Wedgwood were made. The manufactory was blown up by Lord Hill during the Peninsular War (1812).

In the meantime in France patents for the manufacture of porcelain had been granted to Louis Poterat, "Le Sieur de St. Etienne," and to Reverend of Paris. While there are examples of the work of both of these men, neither of them succeeded in producing china in commercial quantities, and the specimens can only be regarded as interesting experiments. The first porcelain manufactory in Europe was that of Chicanneau and his son at St. Cloud, established some time prior to 1698. The body was a fine milky white color, very translucent and carefully decorated both with Oriental patterns and in the pure French style. On the death of Chicanneau the works were continued by Henri Trou. They were burned down in 1773 and were not rebuilt. Following this came Lille (1711) and Chantilly (1725). Mennecy-Villeroy (1735) united with Bourg-la-Reine in 1773. Sceaux and

Arras (1711). Of these, Chantilly is the most noteworthy, the glaze being stanniferous, which imparted a special brilliancy and softness to the colors.

Two workmen from St. Cloud, under the patronage of the Marquis Orry de Fulvy, started a manufactory at Vincennes in 1740, which only escaped failure by the intelligence of a workman named Gravant. The King of France became interested in this manufactory, and though up to 1749 the expenses had exceeded the income, the porcelain manufactured there had become of considerable repute, especially the vases decorated with flowers in relief. Some exquisite colors had been realized, including the *bleu de roi* and *Rose Pompadour*. Boucher and Vanloo supplied designs for figures and groups which were beautifully reproduced in biscuit. In 1753 the King owned one-third of the shares and authorized the employment of his monogram as a mark. The premises were found too small for the growing business, and in 1756 were moved to the new manufactory at Sèvres. This then was the birth of a pottery which extended more influence than any other similar institution in the world and early specimens of which are most highly prized by connoisseurs. For one reason, *pate tendre* was a distinct invention; the Meissen china was a successful reproduction of an Oriental body. For another, owing to the softness of the glaze, the colors sank in it and lost the applied appearance they have on hard porcelain.

SEVRES VASE.

The manufacture of *pate tendre* was continued at Sèvres concurrently with that of *pate dure* until 1804, when it was abandoned.

CHAPTER X.

PORCELAIN IN EUROPE; HARD PORCELAIN.

The credit of having made the first hard porcelain in Europe must be awarded to Johann Böttger, or Böttcher, about 1710. Böttger was born in 1681 or 1682 at Schleiz, in the territory of the Reuss. He was apprenticed to an apothecary of Berlin and interested himself in experiments in a search for the philosopher's stone, that ignus fatuus of the alchemists of the day. In some manner he incurred the displeasure of the authorities and fled to Saxony, then under the electorate of Augustus II. This profligate and extravagant King, believing that Böttger knew the secret of transforming the baser metals into gold, tried to wrest

BOTTGER STONEWARE.
FROM "AMERICAN HOMES & GARDEN."

the secret from him, but bearing in mind that only a little time previously the King had sent to execution one Klettenburg for failing in the same direction, Böttger denied the implication. But the King was not satisfied and insisted that Böttger should experiment with that end in view. It was then that, needing crucibles capable of withstanding great heat, he made some experiments with a red clay and succeeded in producing a body so dense that it could be cut only on a lapidary wheel. The King saw this and in it a resemblance in texture to the Chinese porcelain of which he was an enthusiastic collector, having spent over a million dollars on it for the decoration of his Japanese palace. So Böttger was sent to the laboratory of Count Tschirnhaus, who was experimenting in pottery and who we know had been in communication with John Dwight, of Fulham. The two continued their experiments and that these might be conducted with more secrecy they were transferred to the castle of Albrechtsburg at Meissen. This red stoneware was a substantial improvement over anything that had been made in Europe up to that time. The Elector gave them all possible assistance. Fischer, a Dresden artist, and père Egelbert, of Delft, with other workmen from Holland, were called in, ovens were constructed and the *Bastion de la Jeune Fille* where they were housed became the cradle of the Royal manufactory of Saxony.

A KAENDLER GROUP.   MARCONI PERIOD.

During the invasion of Saxony by Charles XII of Sweden, Böttger was sent for safety to Konigstein. In 1707 he returned to Dresden and in the following year Tschirnhaus died, leaving Böttger to continue the fight alone. The red body had been much improved and large quantities of it seem to have been made. It is almost identical to the red stoneware of the Chinese and that made by the Elers brothers in England. Much of it was decorated with gold leaf in Japanese designs. It was called red porcelain, though the secret of real porcelain seemed as far off as ever. A fortunate series of events at last placed the secret in Böttger's grasp. John Schnorr, a rich ironmaster, when out riding near Aue noticed that his horses' hoofs stuck repeatedly in a soft white earth and it occurred to him that it might be utilized as a powder for dressing wigs, then an important article of commerce. The idea proved to be successful and some of it eventually came into Böttger's hands. He immediately recognized it for what it was, kaolin, and the secret was practically solved. His experiments confirmed this and a period of intense excitement followed. The King saw in it a veritable El Dorado. To a man who spent six million dollars on a fête to one of his mistresses, some such thing was needed. His subjects could bleed for him no longer, for their blood was all exhausted. So the manufactory at Meissen was established and Böttger was appointed director. The exportation of the clay was prohibited, it was carried to the factory in sealed barrels by persons sworn to secrecy; the pottery was a complete fortress; the portcullis was only raised when the secret password was given, an oath of secrecy was taken by all and renewed every month. In every room was painted the ominous words:

Geheim bis ins Grab.

(Be secret unto death.) Böttger was virtually a prisoner. But he had indomitable courage, a cheerful disposition and an immense capacity for work. Success did not come at once, the first pieces being thick and muddy and without glaze. But sufficient progress had been made by 1715 to open a depot in Dresden and to send a quantity of it for sale to the Leipsic fair. The designs were at first applied in mastic oil, but enamel colors were used about three years later. Shapes and decorations were copies or suggestive of the Oriental porcelain. For the King's use Böttger made pieces in low relief pierced at the sides and Augustus must have found his pottery a splendid source of revenue, for the King of Poland is said to have purchased from him six large vases, paying for them with a regiment of dragoons. Arrears of salary to court officials were liquidated by small pieces of porcelain and the King promised to enoble Böttger, a reward the libertine apparently forgot all about. The intense application to work, the confinement of the castle pottery, undermined Böttger's health and he died in 1719 at the age of thirty-seven. He was succeeded in the directorate by Harold and the manufactory began to prosper, especially after 1730, the number of persons employed being 378 in 1750, against 33 in 1720. Painters and modelers of ability were employed and their influence was quickly felt. Among them was the sculptor Kaendler, whose figure pieces from their grace and beauty did much to enhance the fame of Meissen. His work dates from 1731. Lindner, the most celebrated of the Meissen artists, painted birds and insects from 1725 to 1745. The Oriental style had by this time been practically exhausted.

From 1731 to 1733 Augustus II assumed the management and from 1733 to 1756 it was vested in Count Bruhl, almost as great a profligate as his master. The seven years' war—1756-1763—almost put an end to the Saxon pottery, its whole store of china being seized by the victorious enemy and sold for $86,400. Frederic the Great almost denuded it of workmen, whom he sent to the factory at Berlin. A herculean attempt was made by Helbig to maintain the factory during that critical period, notwithstanding the fact that over three hundred and ninety-eight thousand dollars' worth of merchandise was taken by the enemy during that period. After peace was proclaimed the pottery recovered its position, but the style had degenerated and Dietrich (born 1712, died 1774), the court painter, was made director. Among other sculptors and artists employed by him was Acier, whose figures and groups equaled and in some respects surpassed those of Kaendler. The well-known antique figures and groups were produced at this time. After Dietrich's death came another period of decadence. In 1796 Count Marcolini was appointed director and continued until 1814. A more classical style was adopted, imitated from the French, and pieces of this period, marked with the swords and star beneath, are highly esteemed. Bergrath Oppal was director from 1814 to 1833, but the quality of the production again deteriorated, Meissen had lost its prestige and gradually sank in importance and for a long period did but counterfeit its previous successes. In 1827 Kuhn, the then director, succeeded in making liquid gold, which was at least a great financial success, but that is about all that can be said in its favor. In 1850 coal was first used for firing. In 1863 the factory was transferred to the Triebischthal, near Meissen, as it was feared the engines would be disastrous to the beautiful halls of the Albrechtsberg. This new factory was enlarged in 1863 and again in 1873. After the death of Kuhn the oberfactor Raithel was made director, and the manufactory owes much of its present prosperity to his successful direction. He was succeeded in 1894 by H. C. Brunnemann. Thanks to the ability of Professor Sturm, whatever prestige Meissen may have lost has been fully regained. The exhibit at Paris in 1900, and at subsequent exhibitions, shows the wonderful change that has taken

PLACQUE BY PROFESSOR STURM.

place. The art is more robust and virile, new methods have been thought out and their application showed some unique results. The *pate-sur-pate* and *grand feu* pieces by Professor Sturm, the groups and figure paintings by Andresen and the decorations by Guiot and Hentschel demonstrated this. Professor Ernst Zimmermann is the present director.

Meissen porcelain is often spoken of as Dresden or Saxon china, the terms expressing the same thing. The best known mark is the crossed swords and it has perhaps been more extensively imitated than any other.

Notwithstanding the rigorous measures taken to confine the secret of the manufacture of porcelain to Meissen, the matter was of such paramount interest and importance that it was inevitable that sooner or later it should leak out, and such was the case. As early as 1718 a manufactory was established at Vienna by Du Pasquier, who secured the services of a man named Stenzel from the Meissen works. But he evidently knew very little, for after a few years he returned to Meissen. The pottery languished until 1744 when it was bought by the State, the Empress Maria Theresa extending her patronage to it and matters considerably improved.

In 1784 it was under the direction of Baron von Sorgenthal and it was then that the fine works that have made it famous were produced. The beautiful colors invented by the chemist, Leithner, have never been surpassed, although the paste was not as good as that of Meissen. The best of these were a rich cobalt blue and a brown red. A fine staff of artists was engaged, the works of such artists as Angelica Kaufman and Watteau were beautifully reproduced and enriched with the fine gilding for which Vienna is famous. Good imitations of Wedgwood ware were produced under the direction of Flaxman and the works were at their best until 1820. George Perl, a distinguished decorator, succeeded Leithner and in 1856 Alexander Lowe assumed the directorship. It was during this period in 1864 that the works were permanently closed by a decision of the Reichstag. The Austrian shield was used as a trade-mark and from 1784 to 1864 the last three numerals of the year are embossed in the clay.

Other places where escaping workmen carried the secret of the composition of porcelain and established factories were: Anspach (Bavaria), in 1718, where copies of Rouen faience designs were made; Bayreuth (Bavaria), 1720, where stoneware ornamented with figures and medallions had previously been made; Höchst, near Mayence (Germany), 1720, where a workman named Ringler carried the secret, of which he was subsequently robbed when drunk, by other workmen. There was already a faience manufactory there whose products are much prized and many of the designs were reproduced in porcelain. The factory is celebrated for its violet red color, for the figures and groups of Melchior and in a lesser degree for those of his successor, Reis, which are known as "thick heads," all his figures having abnormally large heads. A figure of a lady playing a xylophone of Höchst porcelain brought $1,300 at a sale in Berlin Berlin in 1909. In 1794 General Custine destroyed the manufactory, but some molds and models were saved and afterwards used by a potter named Dahl, who continued to use the trade-mark of the original pottery.

The factory at Berlin was founded in 1750 by Wegley, who secured the services of some potters from Höchst. Professor Binns states that "the proprietor, Edward Cave, was one of the original shareholders in the works at Worcester." In 1763 the factory passed into the hands of the King of Prussia and we have seen how during the war with Saxony he drafted large numbers of workmen from Meissen to Berlin and by their aid the ware was brought to great perfection. To assist the development of the works an edict was issued prohibiting any Jew from marrying until he could show that he had bought a certain quantity of china. Lithophanies, or transparencies, were invented here. The Berlin porcelain is highly esteemed, especially for use in the chemical laboratory, the factory has always been progressive and is to-day producing work of a very high order under the directorship of Dr. Heinicke, who has associated with him Professor Schmutz-Baudiss, whose beautiful work has attracted so much attention in the past few years. The pieces of crystallized glaze made at Berlin are especially noteworthy. Professor Kips is the art director, and Wanzel and Trzaska the best known of a large staff of artists.

At Frankenthal, Hannong of Strasburg, started a factory in 1755, which, after passing to his son in 1759, came into the possession of the Elector, Carl Theodore, in 1761, who greatly improved the quality of the production. It was closed in 1800. The productions are known as Carl Theodore china. An attempt was made at Fürstenburg by the Duke of Brunswick in 1746 to make porcelain, but it was not until six years later that any success was attained and then only by the aid of workmen from Höchst. The pottery is still in existence and has recently executed a presentation service with views of Brunswick for the Duke Regent of Brunswick.

Nymphenburg was founded in 1754 by the elector of Bavaria, some Vienna workmen being engaged, and in 1758 Duke Carl of Wurtemburg founded a factory at Ludwigsburg with the assistance of Ringler. The Nymphenburg factory is still in existence and has lately produced some charming groups of poultry and similar subjects.

In Italy Francesco Vezzi started a pottery at Venice in 1749 and was ennobled by the Senate, the clay being procured from Saxony. After his death in 1740 it ceased to exist. In 1758 Hewelcke, a German, was granted the privilege of making porcelain and a second one was granted in 1762 to a rival potter, upon which Hewelcke returned to Germany. In 1765 Cozzi started a porcelain works, using clay found near Venice, and conducted a successful business until 1812, when the works were closed.

Russian porcelain is treated of under the name of that country.

In Sweden, the pottery at Rörstrand, near Stockholm, which had been in existence for a few years as a faience manufactory, commenced to make porcelain about 1730, under the direction of Conrad Hunger, a Meissen decorator, but it was not until about 1745 that the products attained a certain degree of perfection.

In Belgium, Peternyck, a native of Lille, France, in 1751 obtained the privilege of making porcelain in Tournay. English workmen constituted the bulk of the force. The bleu de roi produced here equaled that of Sèvres.

It is now necessary to revert to France. The Sèvres factory accepted the services of two Meissen potters, Busch and Stadelmeyer, in order to make the natural porcelain, but after long and costly experiments the attempt was abandoned and they were discharged, as to manufacture it necessitated the use of the German kaolin, and its cost and that of its transportation rendered it impossible to compete with the Saxon china.

Kaolin of an impure character was discovered at Hestre, in France, and some experiments were made with it, and it was abandoned. Count de Brancas-Lauraguaise, however, in 1764 continued these experiments on his own account, and there are several specimens in existence. We find that two years later, 1766, he was in England and possibly worked at Chelsea, taking out in that year a patent for hard or natural china, which antedated Cookworthy's patent by two years.

In 1765 a most fortunate accident rendered France in a position to produce natural porcelain, for Madame Darnet, the wife of a poor surgeon, found near St. Yreix a soft earth, which on account of its oily nature she thought she could use as a substitute for soap, and which, upon analysis, proved to be the much desired kaolin. Great a boon as this proved to Limoges and France in general, that country did not prove itself very grateful to Madame Darnet, for up to 1825 she was spending her old age in poverty, when through the intervention of M. Alluaud and others Louis XVIII granted her a pension.

The first two potteries started as a result of this discovery were the one at La Seynie by the Marquis de St. Aulaire and the Comte de la Seynie, and that of Gabriel Grellet in Limoges about 1773 or 1774. Marryatt states that Grellet supported by Minister Turgot was granted permission to export his porcelain without duty, the mark to be "C. D." Pieces with this mark in rough script are known, but no meaning can be ascribed to them. In 1784 his fabrique was purchased by the king as a branch manufacture of Sèvres. Grellet was director and Massier controller. It may here be mentioned that Sieur Massier had a faience factory in Limoges, established in 1737. An inferior kaolin was introduced and Grellet resigned in 1785 and was replaced by Alluaud, who sacrificed his private fortune to the improvement of the works. He was appointed Director of the Mint and Massier provisionally succeeded him in 1793-5. The works were subsequently purchased by Joubert and Cancate. In 1794 M. Monnierie established in the old Augustine Convent a manufacture which continued in operation until 1800, when it declined and was later turned into a carpet manufactory. Baignol, of the La Seynie works, left there and shortly after set up on his own account in Limoges the largest works there with the exception of the one founded in 1797 by Alluaud Père, which was carried to great perfection by his son. "Alluaud porcelain," writes Mr. Marryatt, "was distinguished for its whiteness and the brightness of its enamel. * * * His manufacture, which rose in the storms of the Revolution, was remarkable for the rapidity of its progress." The porcelain made at Limoges was sent to Paris to be decorated, and while Marryatt mentions the decorated ware of Alluaud we are of the opinion that following the usual custom it had been decorated in Paris. If any decorations were attempted in Limoges the amount was inconsiderable, and it was left to an American, David Haviland, to initiate in 1839 the decoration of services for the table, the story of which will be told later. Other early Limoges potters were Ruaud, Pierre Tharaud and Michel & Volin.

ALEX. BRONGNIART.

At Sèvres the illustrious Alexander Brongniart, who was director from 1800 to his death in 1847, sold off all the undecorated pâte tendre in 1804, so enthusiastic was he over the kaolinic or hard porcelain. France and the pottery world in general owe a deep debt of gratitude to this distinguished chemist, who, by his disinterestedness, his ability and influence succeeded in putting in order the affairs of the manufactory and made it self-supporting until the year 1804, when it became crown property and was managed for the Emperor. His honesty and ability were recognized by the successive governments which ruled France during his tenure of office, perhaps the most prosperous in the annals of Sèvres. Two enduring monuments perpetuate his memory, his "Traité des Arts Céramiques" and the Museum at Sèvres, which he founded in 1823. Under his scientific direction the processes were much improved; vases 7 feet 10 inches high were made, painted with compositions intended to glorify the chief events in the career of Napoleon I. Practically every piece was so designed; triumphal char-

78 SÈVRES.

iots, statues of Fame, Egyptian monuments, sumptuous table services with borders of war trophies and painted centers of battle scenes; life-size busts of the Emperor and Empress, and table tops. We may well question the taste displayed and think it

MODERN SEVRES.

somewhat ridiculous, but they are saved from absolute failure by the perfection of their execution. Brongniart was succeeded by Ebelman, and during his directorship the pâte-sur-pâte process was introduced by Louis Robert (about 1850), but the experiments were so long and costly that it was not until 1862 that Sèvres was able to send to the London Exhibition a set of small cups, painted with subjects from La Fontaine's fables. The process consists of painting with clay instead of color, white on a colored ground, the modeling being produced by transparency, according to the thickness of the paste, very beautiful cameo-like effects being produced. The process was fraught with danger, the losses were excessive, but these were greatly minimized by the persevering efforts of Alphonse Salvetat, the distinguished chemist of Sèvres, who died in 1882. M. Solon-Miles, now known as M. L. Solon, was the principal artist in this beautiful work.

Ebelman died in 1852 and was succeeded by Victor Regnault, who retired soon after the breaking out of the Franco-German War in 1870, and was followed by Louis Robert, head of the artistic department. He died in 1882 and was succeeded by M. Lauth.

During the reign of Louis Philippe the vases, tables, etc., were overloaded with sculptured relief ornaments, the painting, gilding and ground completely obscuring the beauty of the china, but in 1852 under the direction of M. Dieterle, the general style of decoration was improved and the paintings no longer covered the whole of the surface.

Theodore Deck was director from 1887 to 1891 and was succeeded by M. E. Baumgart. The ceramics of M. Deck had already established him as the foremost ceramist of Europe, he having succeeded in reproducing all the so-called lost arts of pottery in his Paris factory, which he founded in 1859.

In 1884 a new kind of porcelain with a kaolinic base and a soft glaze was invented and the same year produced some beautiful reds of copper and colored enamels rivaling those of the Chinese.

The commercial condition, however, of the manufactory had for some time been deplorable, the year 1894 showing a deficit of 105,617 francs. In 1897 M. Chaplain, who succeeded M. Baumgart, resigned in disgust and an inquiry into the commercial and artistic depreciation of Sèvres was ordered. The exhibition of 1900 was sufficient proof that so far as the artistic part was concerned Sèvres had resumed her old position as the leader in the ceramic world. Abandoning the traditional output the manufacture of grès was invested with a dignity which might be almost termed royal; flammé reds were successfully produced in vases 4 feet 7 inches high, which, considering the difficulty of firing, is a remarkable achievement. Crystalline glazes, exquisite pieces of grand feu underglaze painting and works in pâte-sur-pâte testified to this renaissance of Sèvres and form a monument to the ability of the splendid corps of painters and sculptors who are responsible for them.

The success of Sèvres and the discovery of kaolin in several French provinces led to the establishment of manufactories in all parts of the country. In some, if not all, respects these all imitated Sèvres both in the manufacturing processes and the appropriation of shapes and patterns. As Chinese porcelain had been the model of the earlier manufactories, that of Sèvres served the same purpose to the secondary ones. In Paris the first one was in the Faubourg St. Lazare, 1772, by Paul Hannong, followed by the Manufactorie de la Courtille (1773), afterwards purchased by Pouyat of Limoges. Clignancourt (1775) produced the most perfect porcelain of that period and nearly approaching it was that of *Porcelain a la Reine* (1778), patronized by Marie Antoinette. Early in the nineteenth century Guy & Housel controlled this manufactory. Guerhard & Dehl, the latter an able chemist, founded the works in the Rue de Bondy in 1789, its products being known as *Porcelaine du Duc d'Angoulême*. There was also a manufactory patronized by the Duke of Orleans (1784); one owned and managed by Nast, and another by an Englishman named Potter, who later was the first in Paris to manufacture English earthenware. The rise of Limoges with its advantageous manufacturing facilities was the death knell of the Parisian potters, and in the early part of last century Paris only retained a monopoly of the decoration of the porcelain made in Limoges.

In the provinces Niederwiller and Lille were the most important. The former was under the direction of the Baron de Beyerlé from 1768 to 1780. In 1793 Gen. Count de Custine became the owner and

VASE IN WEDGWOOD STYLE
BY NAST, PARIS, A. D.
1780-1835.

was succeeded by Lanfrey, the former manager. At Lille coal was first used for firing, superseding wood in 1785. The product of both these factories almost equaled that of Sèvres. Joseph Robert at Marseilles made excellent porcelain, often decorated with sea pieces. Valenciennes, founded in 1785, made a reputation with its bisque statuettes and groups. Caen had a porcelain works founded in 1798, but notwithstanding the excellence of its productions it only existed a short time. There were also two manufactories at Orleans and porcelain was made at the Choisy-le-Roi pottery.

CHAPTER XI.
ENGLAND.

ROMAN POTTERY—ENCAUSTIC TILES—JOHN DWIGHT—SLIP PAINTING—DELFT—THE ELERS—SALT GLAZE—ASTBURY—LIVERPOOL—ROCKINGHAM.

Of all modern nations the potters of England have exercised more influence in ceramics than those of any other country. While England borrowed freely from every available source, her potters were never content to become mere slavish imitators, but impressed with their own individuality whatever they had appropriated. Salt glaze stoneware was a German invention, but it was in Staffordshire that it obtained its development. It was the English hard flint earthenware that changed the manufacture of ware for domestic purposes the world over, and the introduction of bones in China gave a body which has never been surpassed. Nor was the activity of the English potter confined to his own country. One of the first of the potters of Delft was an Englishman, Tom Jones, and many of the French potteries were founded by English potters. He also invaded Sweden, Spain, Italy and Germany. The pottery business in this country is, or rather was, distinctively English. Bennett built the first pottery in East Liverpool, and his contemporary, Croxall, was an Englishman, too.

The primitive pottery of England did not vary much from that of other embryonic nations. That of the ancient Briton consisted mostly of cinerary urns made of coarse clay mixed with sand and probably fired in the funeral pyre. The higher civilization introduced by the Romans was responsible for a greater development of the art. The potter's wheel came into use; glaze was introduced, and the ware fired in regularly constructed kilns. The pottery varied considerably in character at the three great centers of production, viz., the Upchurch Marshes in Kent, on the River Nen in Northumberland and the Salopian potteries. The Upchurch ware was either bluish-black or drab, graceful in form and ornamented with incised lines or dotted figures. The Castor or Durobrivian ware of the Nen was even more carefully thrown than that of Upchurch and was decorated with slip figures and ornaments. The Salopian ware was of two kinds, the one white, the other a light red. In addition to these three centers, pottery was made in many other localities. The Anglo-Saxon failed to carry on the achievements of the Romans and had apparently an aversion to pottery for domestic purposes, using wood for bowls and horn for drinking vessels, but continued the use of it for cinerary urns. This apathy to the fictile art seems to have continued for centuries, and one must pass to the fourteenth century before finding anything worthy of notice. At this period and possibly a century earlier beautifully designed and potted encaustic or inlaid flooring tiles were made by monastic orders, and their manufacture continued until the seventeenth or eighteenth century. The art was probably brought from Europe, but nowhere did it attain greater dignity than in England. The design was first impressed in the clay and the depression filled in with clay of another color. The difficulty of regulating the composition of these clays so that they should shrink equally during firing was no mean task, but was successfully accomplished, while the designs were of infinite variety. Many beautiful pavements of these encaustic tiles are in existence to-day and can be seen in Westminster Abbey, Ely Cathedral, Chertsey Abbey and many other ecclesiastical buildings. While there are a few examples of jugs, etc., which have been cautiously ascribed to the same source, the monks do not appear to have availed themselves of their knowledge of clays to attempt an impetus in pottery for household purposes, and if we except the green glazed pieces ascribed to the reign of Elizabeth (1558-1603) and the "gray-beards" of James I (1603-1625) we have again nothing worthy of note until we come to the Fulham stoneware of John Dwight (1671). Little or nothing was known of this Father of English pottery until 1862, when twenty-eight pieces which had been preserved by his descedants passed into the possession of Mr. Baylis, who wrote an account of them in the *Art Journal*. A subsequent discovery of further specimens and much valuable documentary matter threw further light on his productions and methods. M. Solon says: "The mythological figures in imitation of bronze are especially remarkable; the 'Jupiter' of the Liverpool museum and the 'Meleager' of the British Museum are worthy of an Italian artist of the Renaissance." Dwight was a man of education and must have been a person of considerable importance, for we find he was in communication both with the Elers brothers and Count Tschirnhaus. He occupies the position of having made not only the first stoneware made in England, but the first pottery to successfully rival the foreign wares on which the English had had to rely, and his name should be held in as high honor as that of any of the illustrious English potters who followed him. Considering the times in which he lived, he relatively achieved more, and his influence on English pottery cannot be overrated. The Fulham pottery was continued by Dwight's descendants until 1862.

FULHAM STONEWARE.

The manufacture of stoneware thus initiated spread to the Midland counties, and that of the brown variety become localized at Nottingham, Chesterfield and Derby. It was there that the black bear jugs were originated and also the jugs and mugs the handle of which was formed as a greyhound. The Fulham ware was largely imitative of Germany models, but the uneducated potters of the Midlands struck a more original note with their plain and unpretending shapes.

Slightly antedating and contemporary with the introduction of stoneware in England was the production of the distinctively English slip painted ware. The Romans had used this style of ornamentation in England, but whether there was any connection between the two has not been demonstrated. The decoration is applied through the medium of a little spouted vessel filled with slip, to the spout of which various sized quills are attached, and through these quills the slip is allowed to trail on the ware in the pattern desired by the potter. The piece was usually further embellished with a number of small knobs—Wrotham in Kent furnishes the earliest dated example, 1656. The Wrotham ware is generally overloaded with ornament and is often inscribed with the name of the place. The industry did not last there very long, but spread to Cheshire and Derbyshire and finally found its best expression in Staffordshire. Thomas and Ralph Toft are the names best known there in connection with it. The articles principally made were Posset pots, tygs, piggins, cradles, candlesticks, jugs and large dishes. Posset is a mixture of hot ale, milk, sugar and spices, with dice of bread or oatcake, the tyg, a tall cup with many handles; the piggin, a shallow vessel with a long handle at one side, used for ladling out the liquor brewed in the tyg. These tygs were made at Wrotham before being made in Staffordshire, but they were only so called in the latter place. It is probably a corruption of the Anglo-Saxon *tigel*, a tile, a brick, anything made of clay, a pot, a vessel. Cradles were made for presentation purposes, and it is still the custom to present a cradle, usually of silver, to the Mayor or other official, on the birth of a child during his tenure of office. This slip painting, crude as it was, was the expression of a rude art by men who had nothing but their own initiative to depend upon, and is valuable as being the prototype of the exquisite pâte-sur-pâte decoration of the present day.

STAFFORDSHIRE TYG.

The success of Delft was an incentive to the English potter to produce similar wares, and there are small wine jars said to be of English make, one of which is dated 1652. But the first official record is of a patent granted to John Arians van Hamme in 1676, for making "porcelain after the way practiced in Holland" at Lambeth. Quite a colony of potters eventually congregated here, there being at one time as many as twenty potteries.

SLIP DECORATED CRADLE.

A POTTERY PRIMER.

From Lambeth the art—if such it may be called—extended to Bristol, Liverpool and Staffordshire. The articles made were principally for utilitarian purposes, if we except some large round dishes usually called blue dash chargers. These latter were coarsely painted with figure subjects, mostly celebrated personages of the time. Much of the decoration was applied with a sponge, and around the edge blue is roughly daubed on. The English Delft at best could not compare with that of Holland. The glaze, or enamel rather, was poor in color and uneven, the body often showing through. The work was in the hands of, for the most part, ignorant persons, and unlike the slip-painted ware, it was not the expression of an uncultured craftsman, but a poor imitation of a commercial article and apparently never rose above this. The best was made at Liverpool. In Staffordshire the local product prevented it taking any firm hold, and the former gradually superseded it. In this instance the English potter failed to improve on an adapted process, neither impressing it with his own individuality nor adding the least discovery for its improvement.

ELERS WARE.

The advent of the Elers brothers in England was perhaps more far reaching in its influence for good than any other circumstance connected with English pottery. John Philip and David Elers came of a noble family of Saxony. Their father had been Ambassador to several European courts and also served a term as burgomaster of Amsterdam. When William of Orange was invited to become King of England, in 1688, the Elers came in his train. The King granted a pension of £300 a year to their sister, but there is no record that he extended his patronage beyond this. David set up a pottery store in London. John

Philip went to Staffordshire and founded a pottery there. We do not know the date of his arrival, but he had long been at work in 1698. This pottery was situated at a lonely spot called Bradwell Wood, near to Burslem. At that time there were some eighteen or twenty potteries at Burslem, whose productions consisted mostly of butter pots. We have called them potteries, though most of them had but one kiln, and the working force consisted usually of the potter and the members of his family. These butter pots were finished at one fire and were sent mostly by pack horse to Uttoxeter market. If the potter was a freeholder of Burslem he had a right to take what clay or coal he wanted from any unenclosed or unenfranchised land, and the sides of the lanes and often as not a hole in the street furnished all he needed of both. Many of these holes were in existence as late as 1825. Rude as were their lives and products, we shall see that there was a longing for something better, an intangible desire for improvements.

The Elers brought with them—if indeed David ever took any share in the pottery work—new methods, artistic taste and culture. It is scarcely to be wondered at that they kept aloof from their fellow-workers and so zealously guarded their processes that only workmen of the most ignorant type were employed. When the ware was finished it was sent to their storeroom and residence at Dimsdale Hall, an old Elizabethan house about a mile distant, and from there to David's shop in London. There are but few genuine specimens of Elers ware in existence, and these are of a very hard and dense red stoneware with embossed ornaments. This decoration was applied after the piece had been thrown and turned by putting a small bit of clay on the desired place and then impressing a design upon it from an intaglio mold, much the same as we use a seal on sealing wax. The superfluous clay was then carefully removed. All the known specimens are small pieces such as cups and teapots. Their grace and daintiness were nothing short of a revelation to the Staffordshire potter. The introduction of salt glazing in England has been credited to the Elers, mostly on the testimony of a workman named Steel, aged 84, who told Wedgwood that he was among those who ran to the spot when the Burslem potters, eight in number, as narrated in Aitkins' History of Manchester, assembled around the Elers new ovens to protest against the volumes of smoke they emitted. A potter protesting against smoke, however dense, issuing from a kiln seems somewhat ludicrous. Moreover, salt glazing does not produce a dense smoke.

Nor has any specimen of salt glaze that could be identified as Elers make ever been found. Between Bradwell Wood and Dimsdale Elers established communication by means of a line of pipes used as a speaking tube. A few years ago some of these pipes were found and they are not salt glazed. Notwithstanding this, it is quite possible the credit belongs to the Elers, for it was shortly after their advent that the practice came generally into use in Staffordshire. The old story that Palmer, of Bagnall, in 1680, discovered the process through the overboiling of a pot of salt water, which caused the sides of the vessel to become glazed, may be definitely dismissed as untenable. We might just as well credit it to Robinson Crusoe, who was amazed to find the inside of one of his pots after firing it, glazed on the interior and who then remembered it had contained a little sea water.

We have alluded to the fact that Elers employed only the most ignorant workmen, the better to guard against the innovations he introduced becoming known. This fact was taken advantage of by two Burslem potters, Twyford and Astbury. The latter feigned idiocy, and the former by his apparent stolid indifference completely deceived his employer. It must have meant eternal watchfulness for these two men to play their parts so well as to avoid detection. So well did they succeed that they were gradually allowed to see all that was done, and, being men of keen intelligence, there was little that escaped their notice. Having obtained the information they required, and they are said to have worked for Elers for two years, the two men left his employ. We shall meet them again later and find that, whatever may be thought of their conduct on this occasion, Astbury at least partially atoned for it by his independent experiments, the result of which had a lasting influence on English pottery. Of Twyford little is known, though his descendants are large manufacturers of sanitary ware at the present time. Elers left Staffordshire about 1710, going first to Chelsea and afterward to Dublin, but he did not again engage in the manufacture of pottery.

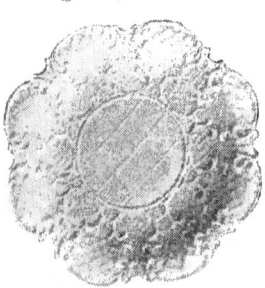

SALT GLAZE PLATE.

This new pottery made by Elers was almost identical with that made by Böttcher some years later. Both are described as porcelain before that word had a more specific meaning, each lacking the important qualification of translucency, and they are more properly termed stoneware.

About this time the process of glazing with salt became general in Staffordshire, and a very marked improvement took place. Instead of the heavy German stoneware, the English potter produced articles of extreme lightness, it being his effort to create something that should rival the Oriental ware and replace the clumsy Delft. When specimens of this beautifully made, salt-glazed stoneware first came to the notice of collectors it was erroneously called Elizabethan ware. Many of these pieces were made in copper or lead molds, which were made so as to stamp both back and front at the same time, and by this means pieces as thin as wafers were made. Others were cast in pitcher or terra-cotta molds, as plaster molds had not then been used in Staffordshire. These pitcher molds always gave clean and well-cut copies, but the castings was tedious. The mold, being filled

ENAMELED SALT GLAZE.   ASTBURY WARE.

with slip, was immediately emptied, leaving a thin coating of clay on the sides. When this was nearly dry it was again filled and emptied, and this was repeated until the necessary thickness of clay was obtained. When sufficiently dry the mold was taken apart and the piece removed. This salt-glaze ware resulted in a great extension of trade; the potteries were enlarged; larger kilns built to keep pace with what had now become an important industry. Astbury and Twyford took the lead, and others identified with it were Thomas and John Wedgwood. In addition to these stamped and cast pieces, much was thrown on the wheel and afterward turned and ornaments "sprigged" on—that is, a small design was made from a mold and fastened on with slip,

About 1750 this salt-glaze ware was decorated in colors fired in the muffle kiln. The manufacture spread to Jackfield, Leeds, Liverpool and Swansea.

With this marked advance the English potter, far from sitting down in contentment, was only spurred on to fresh endeavor. All kinds of clays were eagerly tested for the hitherto unattainable white body, and this was accomplished when Astbury, in 1720, discovered the use of flint, and Booth thirty years later introduced the practice of dipping the ware in an improved glaze held in suspension in water. This was the foundation of the manufacture of English earthenware, an industry which has spread all over the world. Whieldon (1740-1798) greatly improved its quality. While white local clay had been used for the manufacture of pipes, it had not been used for ware for domestic purposes, as the galena which was used for glazing gave it a dirty grayish appearance, so that Astbury's and Booth's discoveries were necessary for its fulfillment.

Agate ware, a distinctly English production, was first made by Dr. Thomas Wedgwood (1731), son of Thomas Wedgwood of the Overhouse Works, Burslem. In this the marbling instead of being on the surface runs through the body and is made by blending together different colored clays and then transversely cutting the mass in thin slices, which are then carefully pressed in the mold. When glazed with blue the hue of agate was imparted to them. Both Astbury and Whieldon produced this ware to perfection.

Ralph Shaw, of Burslem, introduced the slip kiln, and in firing used bits of stoneware so that pieces placed one inside the other could not stick together, leading to the introduction of the stilts now used for that purpose. Failing in the courts to sustain the validity of a patent he had taken out, he emigrated to France and was probably one of the Englishmen who, in 1775, started the manufacture of English earthenware at Montereau.

In 1740 Thomas and John Wedgwood, one a fireman, the other a dipper, established themselves at Burslem. Their experiments with clay were beneficial to the whole community, for they succeeded in classifying their qualities, both good and bad, and henceforth some kind of system could be observed, which resulted in a general all-round improvement.

Thomas Whieldon, whom we have before alluded to, commenced business some time prior to 1740 in a small way at Fenton,

CLOUDED WARE JUG BY WHIELDON

and by his skill as a potter became the leading manufacturer of the time. His productions were extremely various, including the well-known tortoiseshell, which, though made by many other manufacturers, is usually spoken of as Whieldon ware. The same might almost be said of the Cauliflower and Melon ware, of which such large quantities were made. The body had now become so much improved that the potter turned his attention more particularly to shapes, with a view to best display its qualities, and the modelers of the time seem to have derived their inspiration largely from nature, leaves, pineapples, etc., being much used. Whieldon must have been a man of great discrimination in the selection of his apprentices, for Josiah Spode, Robert Garner, J. Barker and William Greatbach all became well-known potters. Wedgwood's ability he also recognized and made a partnership agreement with him for five years. We know that it was Wedgwood who compounded the green glaze so extensively used, and probably he was responsible for much more during this partnership that tended to Whieldon's renown and the prosperity of the trade.

The introduction of a little cobalt or zaffre in the glaze had made the body much whiter, a discovery of William Littler and Aaron Wedgwood, and this led to the practice of painting in enamel colors. There were no trained hands among the Staffordshire potters for this work, and painters were brought from Holland. When gold was added it was done by means of gold leaf fixed with a hard varnish, and it was not until toward the end of the eighteenth century that the burning in of gold was known in Staffordshire.

Before speaking of Josiah Wedgwood we must briefly consider the advance of the art in other parts of England, having already briefly made mention of the brown stoneware of Nottingham and the Delft ware of Bristol, Liverpool, etc. To the latter city we must turn for the first examples of transfer printing on pottery, one of the most important discoveries ever made in its decoration. It was originally used by Alderman Jansen, of Battersea, on enamels, and in 1750 Sadler & Green, of Liverpool, adapted it to pottery. A cheap and effective style of decoration, its success was instantaneous, and the Staffordshire potters quickly took advantage of it and sent large quantities of their ware to the patentees to be decorated. Among these was Josiah Wedgwood and his successors, who continued to have ware printed there as late as 1799. If all the ware credited to Liverpool was really made there the industry must have been very considerable, even if we only consider the ware made specially for America and mostly commemorative of historical events.

While the Liverpool pottery is seldom marked, an exception must be made to that of the Herculaneum, the word being usually impressed. This pottery was founded about 1793 by Richard Abbey and one Graham, but three years later passed into the

THE BUTCHERS' ARMS, LIVERPOOL.

hands of Worthingham, Humble & Holland, who enlarged the works. Its products were varied and consisted of Queensware, black basaltes, green glaze and printed ware. About 1834 the liver, the crest of Liverpool, was adopted as a trade-mark.

The cream-color ware of Staffordshire was also made at Leeds, two brothers named Green founding a factory there in 1753. It is principally remarkable for its basket and pierced ware which obtained a great vogue. Its printed ware dates from about 1780, and both gold and silver lusters were also made. The Leeds ware was beautifully potted and was of a rich cream color, a little darker than Wedgwood's queensware.

The Rockingham pottery, Swinton, near Rotherham, was founded in 1745, but only made bricks, etc., until 1765, when the manufacture of pottery was commenced. The works are called after Charles, Marquis of Rockingham. It was not, however, until 1796, that what was then called "brown china" was produced. This was the regular cream-color body covered with a rich purple brown glaze, the color being obtained from manganese and a little iron. Brameld was the last owner of the works, which were closed in 1843. The glaze on this Rockingham ware is not uniform, but delicately varied, obtained by dipping it several times, and was of a much higher quality than the Rockingham ware of to-day. Green, of Leeds, had also a pottery at Swinton (founded 1790), its products being almost identical with that of Leeds. In 1796 Ralph Wedgwood joined the firm of Tomlinson & Co. at Ferrybridge, and the name was changed to "Wedgwood & Co." At Sunderland and Newcastle a very coarse purple-gold luster was smeared on the ware, many pieces with transfer prints being disfigured in this way. There were many other places where potteries were established, but their productions do not call for special notice, adding nothing either in novelty or advance to what already existed.

CHAPTER XII.

JOSIAH WEDGWOOD.

In our brief review of Staffordshire pottery we have seen how prominently the name Wedgwood occurs, but it was reserved to Josiah, son of Thomas and Mary Wedgwood, born in 1730, to make it the best known and the greatest in the history of English pottery. His life has been told so many times and told so well that the briefest outline is all we shall give here. We have already seen how much progress had been made through the cumulative discoveries of his predecessors. The native clays had largely been superseded by those of Devon and Cornwall. The body had become hard and compact by the addition of flint; the method of grinding flint in water was known; the whiteness of the glaze had been heightened by the addition of zaffre;

JOSIAH WEDGWOOD, F.R.S.

it was used held in suspension in water instead of being applied as a dry powder, and there was practically nothing to add to the body made by such potters as Whieldon to increase either its utility or beauty.

Josiah was the youngest of the large family of Thomas and Mary Wedgwood, and was born July 12, 1730. His father died in 1739, and Josiah shortly after had to make his start in life with the very rudimentary education with which a year or two of schooling had furnished him. His brother, Thomas, had succeeded to the Churchyard works, and here at an early age he was set to work as a thrower. His skill soon attracted the attention of his fellow workmen so rapid was his progress. In 1741 he had a severe attack of smallpox, which affected his right knee, which never completely healed. For a time he resumed his work as a thrower, but having to sit with his leg extended on a stool before him, it so hampered his position at the wheel that he was obliged to abandon the thrower's bench and went to the molder's board. The ailment of Wedgwood proved a blessing in disguise, for unable to share in the sports of the day he set his mind to studying the laws and secrets of his art. He made experiments with all the clays he could procure and endeavored to find some new way of ornamentation. His brother resented what he looked upon as a loss of time, and though Josiah worked for him as a journeyman after the expiration of his apprenticeship, when at maturity he received the modest competence of £20, bequeathed him by his father, he sought a freer field in which to indulge his aspirations. Accordingly he entered into partnership with a potter, Thomas Alders, and John Harrison, a Newcastle tradesman, who furnished the bulk of the money. The little pottery at Cliff Bank, Stoke-upon-Trent, was, however, only operated for two years, when Harrison withdrew and shortly afterwards it was pulled down. About 1752 Wedgwood's talents were recognized by Thomas Whieldon, of the Fenton Hall Works, the best potter of the day, who took him into partnership. He devoted himself to modeling and improving the various tortoiseshell, agate and cauliflower ware then being produced. It was here that he invented the green glaze which immediately became popular. His knee still affected him and caused frequent absences from the works, and it became necessary to impart the formula of this glaze to others, with the result that it soon became common property. Whieldon retired in 1759, having made a fortune, and the partnership was dissolved. The following year Wedgwood rented a portion of the Ivy House Works, Burslem, from his distant cousins, John and Thomas Wedgwood, at a rental of £10 a year, the working premises consisting of two kilns, a few sheds and the ivy-covered cottage. Here he made his green glaze, his tortoiseshell and perforated plates. Their beauty and careful finish brought their natural reward in the way of increased business. The increase in his working force called for larger premises, so he took the Brickhouse Works, better known as the Bell Works, the site of which is now partly occupied by the Wedgwood Memorial. One of the greatest difficulties that confronted Wedgwood was the carelessness of the workmen, but with infinite patience he at last succeeded in making them appreciate the joy of producing carefully made and finished ware, and turned what had been a crew of roystering workmen into an ardent band of craftsmen. Another difficulty was the transportation of the ware. Roads virtually there were none; they were mere lanes, wretched at all times and utterly impassable in bad weather. Materials were brought from a distance chiefly on pack horses, and the manufactured articles were returned in the same way. The lowest charge was eight shillings a ton for ten miles. The goods were often pilfered on the way, which was infested by highwaymen, and all these things made the conducting of manufacturing extremely hazardous. So Wedgwood busied himself successfully, in a good roads movement, and did not cease his activity until fairly good roads led out of Burslem in all directions and the canal connecting the Trent and the Mersey was an accomplished fact. In the meantime work at the pottery had gone on with surprising vigor, the workmen had now allotted duties instead of being everything in turn, mode of production was simplified, tools were improved and materials were carefully selected. In 1766 Wedgwood took into partnership Thomas Bentley, a Liverpool merchant of good education, artistic taste and polished manners. Again the works had not sufficient capacity, and Wedgwood built new ones, and a house at the village which he founded under the name of Etruria, entering into possession of them in 1769. It was here he invented his celebrated jasper ware, which was first so called in 1776, a year or so after its discovery. There were several shades of blue, lilac, pink, sage green, olive green, yellow and black, the yellow being the least frequent, the colors being produced with metallic oxide. On this were applied designs in relief exactly in the same way used by Astbury and his successors. This "sprigging," as it is termed, is a distinctly English process introduced in Staffordshire by the Elers. At first Wedgwood, following the prevailing taste, copied from casts of engraved gems of Greek or Roman origin, and later worked more directly from the originals, employing the best talent he could secure, not only in adapting designs, but in creating original work. Considering the tremendous vogue this jasper ware had it seems open to comment that the number of copied designs is very largely in excess of original ones. Of the latter those designed by John Flaxman, engaged by Wedgwood in 1775, are the most esteemed. Another celebrated modeler was William Hackwood, whose medallions of Wedgwood and his relations and of many local celebrities are evidently characteristic likenesses. The well-known Portland vase was reproduced by Wedgwood in 1790. Originally fifty copies were issued, and it has since been published at intervals. Its vogue has never been satisfactorily explained. Its shape is certainly clumsy and inelegant, the figures under a microscope show coarseness of texture instead of, as in the original, revealing hidden beauties. Like many more of Wedgwood's jasper pieces it may be termed "dully scholastic." The Egyptian black ware of Wedgwood was a great improvement on that already made and was most successful when ornamented in reliefs in white jasper. It was also decorated on its unglazed surface with enamel colors, a process which notwithstanding its inartisticness is still followed. His red ware, made from the clay at Bradwell Wood, the same as used by the Elers, never equaled in color or fineness of grain that made by these pioneer potters nearly a century earlier. The cream color ware he greatly improved, giving to English earthenware a tremendous impetus. This was decorated in enamels in well-chosen designs, and when Queen Charlotte ordered a service of it, it became known in her

LAMP IN EGYPTIAN BLACK WARE.
WEDGWOOD.

honor as Queensware. Wedgwood was not a chemist, for chemistry as applied to pottery was then an unknown quantity. He was a man of surprising energy, of indomitable will; he had the faculty of gauging public taste and ministering to it. His love for his art dominated him; he recognized its possibilities and strove to accomplish them. The dominant note was perfection of workmanship; no poorly finished piece was allowed to leave his pottery; the concealed parts must be as perfect as the revealed. His improvements were the improvements of the district, for he never took out but one patent, and that one of small importance. We yield to none in our admiration of Wedgwood as

PHAETHON AND THE CHARIOT OF THE SUN.
By. G. Stubbs, R. A., 1783.

a potter and a keen business man, and England and the world owe him a deep debt of gratitude, but the claims of those who preceded him cannot in all fairness be overlooked.

Wedgwood married a distant connection, Sarah Wedgwood, in 1764. Four years later his leg had to be amputated, and henceforth he stumped through life on a wooden leg. His eyesight, too, troubled him greatly, and the tender ministrations and loving care of his wife form a beautiful chapter in their history. He died January 3, 1795, aged 65. A few years previously he had admitted into partnership his three sons, John, Josiah and Thomas, and his nephew, Byerly, under the style of Josiah Wedgwood,

Sons & Byerly. The management was assumed by the latter and continued to his death in 1810. In 1823 the third Josiah Wedgwood entered the firm, to be joined by his brother Francis in 1827, and the firm name was changed to Josiah Wedgwood & Sons. John Boyle, one time partner with Herbert Minton, and Robert Brown, were both partners for a limited term of years. Later the firm consisted of Godfrey, Clement and Lawrence Wedgwood—Clement died in 1889 and Godfrey in 1908. The firm now consists of Lawrence, Cecil, son of Godfrey, and Francis Hamilton, son of Clement.

In 1858 Messrs. Wedgwood were fortunate enough to secure the services of M. Emile Lessore, an artist who at the Royal Sèvres Works had attempted to introduce a more artistic style of decoration than then existed. This caused so much dissention and jealousy among the artists that in 1858 he went to England and entered the service of Mintons, but soon removed to the Wedgwood pottery. His work was and is highly appreciated and sought after by connoisseurs, but the climate not suiting him he returned to France. He continued to produce work for the Wedgwoods until his death in 1876.

About this time Mr. Thomas Allen, a figure painter of force and originality, became art director and his undoubted artistic taste was soon apparent in the productions of the firm. Mr. Allen had previously been connected with Minton's and painted many of the figure subjects on tessera which adorn the South Kensington Museum. The old Etruria pottery stands substantially to-day as Josiah left it, many of the old models are still in use and it is possible to-day to obtain replicas of many of the designs first executed years ago.

CHAPTER XIII.

TURNER—WILLIAM ADAMS—CONTEMPORARIES OF WEDGWOOD.

The success achieved by Wedgwood was an incentive to the other manufacturers of the district to improve their production and not only in England but on the Continent of Europe he had a host of imitators. The classical style then in vogue was adapted by all, and there is in consequence a great similarity between the works of Wedgwood and his school. Some of these were men who had sufficient initiative to produce original works, others did not hesitate to reproduce both Wedgwood's shapes and designs. The same source of inspiration

there was really no occasion for slavish copies. Sir William Hamilton's designs of classic vases and other similar works were open to all, and Wedgwood and his contemporaries freely availed themselves of these sources.

In this school two names stand out preëminently, viz., Turner and Adams. John Turner, of Lane End (1762-1786), made jasper which equaled that of Wedgwood, though made from a different formula, while equal praise may be bestowed upon his black basalts. Adams was a personal friend of Wedgwood, and at one time worked for him, and during that period considerably improved the jasper body. He is many times mentioned by Wedgwood, and always in terms of praise and friendship. He left Wedgabout 1780, fifteen years before the

WILLIAM ADAMS.

death of the latter. The Adams family is one of the oldest connected with the pottery trade in Staffordshire. John Adams, of Burslem, who married in 1654, built the Brick House Works, the first brick house in Burslem, afterwards tenanted by Wedgwood. There were four Staffordshire potters named William Adams, who may be differentiated as follows: William Adams, Greengates, Tunstall, 1745-1805; William Adams, Brick House Works, Burslem, 1748-1831; William Adams, Stoke, 1772-1829; William Adams, Greenfield, 1798-1865.

The first three were cousins, the last two father and son. But it was William Adams, of Greengate, who was the potter *par excellence*. The Adams blue jasper was, if possible, finer in color than Wedgwood's and became known as Adams blue, and is conceded by Miss Meteyard, the biographer of Wedgwood, to be of "extraordinary beauty."

Adams also made fine stoneware, which he invariably finished with a black or brown glaze band. This was highly esteemed, and was often thought worthy of a silver mount. Our illustration will convey some idea of the artistic manner in which the Adams stoneware jugs were made. Adams also invented the Mocha ware, which was largely copied and which was being made by five or six potters in 1820. It had a great vogue at the time and is still made. Its distinguishing feature is a band of colored slip on which has been applied another colored slip of

A POTTERY PRIMER.

VASE, 9½ IN., BLUE AND WHITE JASPER, 1790 PERIOD.

greater density, which spreads out on the slip band in the form of a fibre or tree. The article to be decorated is inverted and both slips must be quite wet. Tobacco juice was employed to make the second slip eat its way into the lower one, but now specially prepared Mocha colors are used, one of which rejoices in the name of "Black Jack."

Among the jasper manufacturers of the eighteenth century two firms have been singled out as little better than pirates, viz., Neale & Palmer and Voyez, the latter being also accused of stamping his ware with Wedgwood & Bentley's name. There seems but little evidence to support this charge. Voyez was a clever modeler, he had worked both for Palmer and Wedgwood, and the same source of inspiration from which Wedgwood drew so largely was open to everyone. Mr. Rathbone, a noted expert on old Wedgwood, says: "None of such forgeries are ever met with, and in no instance is the actual form or even color copied." So there has probably been withheld from these firms the meed of praise to which they were justly entitled. Contemporaries of Wedgwood were Enoch Wood (1783-1818), Job Ridgway, John Davenport, Josiah Spode, Thos. Minton and others, all of whom made their impress on English ceramic art, and whose descendants, except in the case of Davenport, are to the present day carrying on the work for which they laid such strong foundations. We shall defer more extended notices of these houses until we have mentioned the early china fac-

AN 18TH CENTURY BLUE AND WHITE JASPER CUP, WITH SHEFFIELD

tories, which will bring us to the close of the eighteenth century, and the story of both china and earthenware can then be more easily taken up, as few of the leading houses confined themselves to one branch alone. This variety of production is characteristic of the English potters, it not being at all unusual for china, earthenware, stoneware and parian to be made by one firm.

CHAPTER XIV.

ENGLISH CHINA—CHELSEA—BOW—DERBY—WORCESTER—COALPORT MINOR CHINA WORKS—LOWESTOFT—PLYMOUTH—BRISTOL.

This most important part of all English china is prepared by burning bones in contact with the air. During the firing, when the materials begin to combine at a certain heat, the bones, being phosphate of lime, which cannot be destroyed by the silica, melt, without combining, into a sort of semi-transparent enamel, and being intimately mixed in the mass give translucency. Previous to the use of bones the Bow factory used a clay from the Cherokee country, U. S. A., called by the natives *unaker*.

BOW SOUP TUREEN, WHITE.
South Kensington Museum.

The origin of the Bow pottery is uncertain, the first patent of which we have any knowledge being taken out in 1744 by Edward Heylyn, of Bow, and Thomas Frye, of West Ham, Essex. Frye, who was a painter, was manager of the works until 1759, when on account of ill health he resigned. He died in 1762. In 1770 the Chelsea works were bought by William Duesbury, of Derby, and he also acquired the Bow works in 1776. The factory at Derby had been in existence some years prior to 1756, when we know that Duesbury was in partnership with John Heath.

The production of these three potteries did not vary considerably, and it is often difficult to distinguish them, especially after the migration of the workmen from Chelsea and Bow to Derby and the use there of the molds and patterns formerly used in the two potteries.

The existence of China clay in England being unknown, the early English potter desirous of emulating the production of Sèvres and Meissen, like the early French potters, had to compound a body from various ingredients, which led to the designation *artificial porcelain*. We have no definite information respecting the founding of these English china works, but the first dated example is a goat and bee jug marked "Chelsea, 1745." Before the two bearing this mark came to light, this had always been ascribed to Bow, the New Canton works, as they were called. There is a certain excellence of manufacture in this which indicates that the works had been some time established, probably by Dutch workmen, for the first two managers of whom we have any knowledge were Charles Gouyn and Nicholas Spirmont, both undoubtedly of Flemish origin. During the first period of the Chelsea works, up to 1757, the body had considerable translucency, a large amount of glassy frit being used and when held to a strong light exhibits irregularly disposed moonlike discs of greater translucency than the rest. The works were closed during 1758, but resumed in the year following, when the body became phosphatic, that is, it contained bone ash. The important discovery of bones as a constituent part of the body must be credited to the Bow factory, the patent taken out by F. Frye, November 17, 1748, clearly indicating it. This discovery has been generally credited to Josiah Spode, the younger (1797-1800), but erroneously, for in addition to its use at Bow and Chelsea, *The Handmaid of the Arts*, in 1780, gives us a formula for a china body. White sand or calcined flints, finely powdered, 20 pounds; white potash, 5 pounds; bones calcined to perfect whiteness, 2 pounds.

CHELSEA-DERBY, COMPOTIER.

The earlier Chelsea wares, from 1750 to 1780, are considered the best, the inspiration coming from Oriental and Continental sources, sometimes being adaptations, sometimes exact copies, even to the mark underneath. After 1780 or 1790 the simplicity of the former wares ceased and for want of intelligent, artistic direction there was a marked deterioration in all English china. Especially was gold used in such an indiscriminate manner as to amount to sheer vulgarity. Professor Church, in his "English Porcelain," says: "The decoration of old English porcelain is often bad from the want of power and knowledge in the decorator, often from want of feeling, and often from want of training in the sound principles of ornamentation. From one or other of these defects arises bad quality of color and inharmonious arrangements of colors; debasement or misapplication of forms originally good and appropriate; extravagant decoration, especially in the way of overmuch gilding, by which attention is distracted from the more important decorative *motifs* of the pieces; hard and mechanical handling of the brush. * * * Even in the darkest times, however, may be traced now and then a happy gleam of fancy, even a flash of original imagination."

An anchor in relief in a raised oval cartouche is the Chelsea mark found usually on the earlier pieces. An anchor roughly pencilled in gold or colors and varying in size, belongs to the later period and was continued until the close of the works. The anchor was also used by Bow accompanied by a dagger and pieces painted by Frye often bear his initials. An encased triangle was also used and this is found on Chelsea pieces with "Chelsea" in script underneath.

William Duesbury was a painter, or, as he is described, "an enameler," from Longton, and became connected with the Derby pottery in 1756. It must then have been in existence several years, though its origin is very obscure. Beyond published advertisements of sales of the pottery product, including "figures after the finest Dresden models," and the fact that the business had so increased as to necessitate the enlargement of the pottery in 1758, we have very little information about this pottery until 1769 or 1770, when Duesbury became the owner of the Chelsea works and six years later that of Bow. Duesbury died in 1786 and was succeeded by his son William, who managed the works alone until 1798, when he took into partnership Michael Kean, a miniature painter. He died in 1796 and was succeeded by his son, William Duesbury, the third of that name. In 1815 the works were leased to Robert Bloor, who continued them until 1848, when the original business ceased to exist. Bloor was an entirely different type of man to the three Duesburys, who during their administration had been careful not to allow any imperfect pieces to be sold. There was consequently a large accumulation of such pieces and Bloor auctioned these off, both in London and at the pottery, realizing a large sum of money from the sales. It also served to demonstrate how quickly goods could be disposed of in this manner; it was a "get-rich-quick" scheme and there was at once a marked falling off in the finish of the product, resulting, as was inevitable, in the closing of the works.

The successive productions of Derby are known as Derby, Chelsea-Derby, Crown Derby and Bloor Derby. The best available painters and modelers were employed, among the former being William Billingsley, the flower painter, who at one time or another worked at all the principal English china works. He was apprenticed to Duesbury in 1774 and worked at Derby nearly twenty-five years. His work is deservedly very highly esteemed. A large number of statuettes and groups were produced, some richly though not inartistically decorated in colors and gold, but the best were in white biscuit of a high degree of excellence, and in the production of which Derby had no rival. Some of them have exquisite lace work on the dresses similar to those of Dresden. Real lace is dipped in slip and then draped on the unfired figures, the fabric burning away and leaving its counterpart in the delicate porcelain. In breakfast and dessert services a rich blue was frequently used as a ground on which other brilliant enamel colors were superimposed, usually of Japanese character and traced out in gold. The best period of this style belongs to the close of the eighteenth and beginning of the nineteenth centuries. Other services were decorated with flowers, figures, etc., by such artists as Billingsley, Askew and others. These latter were simple in their border designs, sometimes gold leafage on a blue band or simple festoons in pink.

DERBY, DIANA STATUETTE IN WHITE BISCUIT.

Prior to 1848 some of the old employees joined together and put into a common stock what money, skill or tools they possessed and started business under the style of Locker & Co. In 1859 Locker died and the name was changed to Stevenson & Co. and later to Hancock & Co. and is now carried on by Sampson Hancock alone.

In 1877 Mr. Edward Phillips, of the Worcester Porcelain

Co.; Mr. Wm. Litherland, a Liverpool china dealer, and Mr. John McInnes formed a company with a capital of £68,000 to revive the lost glories of Derby. The first works were on the Osmaston Road, but the Derby poor house coming into the market, they purchased it, and converted it into a pottery. It was not, however, until 1880 that it was in working order and old Derby shapes and decorations were produced. Mr. Phillips died in 1881 and Mr. Litherland in 1882 and the active control of the works was vested in Henry Litherland and Edward McInnes. In 1889 the Duke of Devonshire assisted them in procuring permission to use the word Royal and the name is now the Royal Crown Derby

OLD DERBY.
Courtesy of *Keramic Studio*.

Porcelain Co., Ltd. While much that was good of the old Crown Derby has been reproduced, the management have by no means confined their activities to mere reproductions, but much original work is produced, some of it evidence of the finest craftsmanship, and, as a rule, the product compares favorably with anything made by their predecessors.

WORCESTER.

The Worcester factory, or, as it was called, "The Worcester Tonquin Manufactory," had its birth in politics. The Georgian party to increase their voting strength resolved on a manufactory of some description. They came in contact with Dr. John Wall, a clever chemist, and William Davis, an apothecary, who had for some time been engaged in experiments in making china, and the scheme for a china manufactory was launched (1751). Having no kaolin, a frit was used in conjunction with pipe clay, for which

A POTTERY PRIMER.

steatite was afterward substituted. The enterprise was conducted with great secrecy, no visitors were allowed and even the keys of the inner and outer doors were not kept by the same person. The early productions were copies or adaptations of blue and white Nankin patterns of a simple character. In 1756 the invention of printing on biscuit-ware was practiced, having been brought there by Robert Hancock, an engraver of Battersea, though an attempt was made by J. Holdship, one of the original partners, to claim

LILY PATTERN PLATE.

the invention. The printing process was largely used for political purposes, portraits of prominent men of the day finding a ready sale. In dinner ware the Lily pattern was the first one engraved, it having previously been painted and it has uninterruptedly continued in use up to the present day, in itself a sufficient criterion of its excellence. The early transfer prints are noticeable for their fine engraving, which sensibly deteriorated as the practice of coloring them increased. About the year 1764 many Chelsea workmen went to Worcester and their influence soon manifested itself, the products plainly showing the Chelsea influence. The coveted apple green of Sèvres, the rich *bleu de roi* ground with salmon scale markings, the paintings of exotic birds and the elaborate but tasteful gold borders are of this period and bear evidence of a cultivated taste. Dr. Wall died in 1776 and the remaining members of the company continued the manufacture until 1783, when they disposed of the works to their London agent, Thomas Flight. In 1788 George III. with three princesses visited the factory, which then gained the title of the Royal Porcelain Works, a warrant confirmed by Queen Victoria in 1883. Speaking of this period, Professor Church says: "The artistic decadence of the ware began during this period (1783-1793), although the pottery and workmanship remained excellent. But the heavy pseudo-classic form, the labored painting and exuberant gilding that were then in vogue gradually displaced the last traces of the grace, freedom and simplicity of the earlier time. Some changes had been made in the firm consequent on the death of John Flight, in 1791, which only call for mere noting.

Flight & Barr, 1793 to 1807.
Barr, Flight & Barr, 1807 to 1813.
Flight, Barr & Barr, 1813 to 1840.

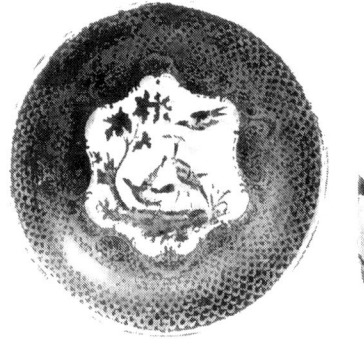

SCALE PATTERN.

This was the last phase of the original Worcester Co., which came pretty near to extinction. In 1786 Robert Chamberlain, the first apprentice Worcester ever had, started in business on his own account and was so successful that the old firm to save itself amalgamated with him in 1840. The partnership was dissolved in 1847, the old factory being closed. In 1850 Mr. F. Lilly and Mr. Kerr became partners and two years later were joined by Mr. R. W. Binns, when Mr. Chamberlain retired and the firm name became Kerr & Binns. In 1862 Kerr & Binns disposed of their business to the present joint stock company, "The Worcester Royal Porcelain Co., Ltd." Mr. Kerr retired and to Mr. Binns

A POTTERY PRIMER.

was intrusted the position of art director, an office he honorably filled until 1897, when, although retaining his seat on the board, he retired from active management.

Among the other productions during the Chamberlain period may be mentioned that of porcelain buttons, which was discontinued on account of some dispute about the machine used for making them and also that of encaustic tiles, the manufacture of which was transferred to Messrs. Maw & Co., of Broseley, in 1851. There is quite a little diversity in the Worcester pastes

MODERN WORCESTER.

which helps to distinguish the various periods, the standard finally adopted being phosphatic similar to the other English china manufacturers. In all the multitudinous productions of Worcester there is one striking characteristic—craftsmanship, the most minute care being bestowed on every little detail and whatever may be the criticisms on patterns or design, there cannot be any on the workmanship. The beautifully embossed patterns rival the best efforts of the Chinese. The enamels of the late Mr. Bott, executed in 1854 and following years, are veritable triumphs of pottery and to-day command large prices. These were mostly executed in white enamel on a rich blue ground. Mr. Bott died in 1870

The jeweled ware of Worcester is considered superior to that of Sèvres, being a more ceramic production. The ivory porcelain (1863) was made the medium for many elegantly shaped vases, etc., which were decorated in bronzes and colored golds and became so popular that the market was flooded with imitations, some with a certain degree of merit, others mere caricatures of the original, but it had the effect of forcing the Worcester Ivory out of the market, at least as far as this country is concerned. The most artistic and successful use of this ivory body was the application of Japanese motifs which have and will be regarded as the best work of this historic house. This and the enamels before referred to are sufficient in themselves to make the administration of Mr. R. W. Binns a memorable one. Worcester has usually been regarded as a "vase" house, though always active in the more utilitarian lines, and at this writing the whole artistic force under the skilful guidance of Mr. E. P. Evans, is concentrated in this direction and at least one notable success has been achieved. This is termed Intaglio. Very chaste designs modeled in low relief are covered with grounds of the most beautiful color, the effect being very rich and charming and distinctly novel. At present this decoration will be confined to service plates, cups and saucers, etc. No less noteworthy is their new Sabrina ware, some lovely effects being obtained by saturating the porcelain with metallic salts, the color from which develops in the fire, occasionally crystallizing and always producing results which cannot be repeated, thus giving it a distinction not otherwise obtainable. These beautiful color effects are used in combination with paintings of birds, etc.

COALPORT.

About the time that the Worcester works were founded a china works was started at Caughley, Shropshire, by a man named Gallimore, though little is known of him. He was succeeded in 1772 by Thomas Turner, of Worcester. An apprentice of the latter, John Rose, started a small pottery at Jackfield further up the river, but soon moved to Coalport, on the opposite bank of the river from Caughley, where there had previously been a small pottery conducted by a man named Young. The pottery was a success from the first and Turner being unable to compete with his young rival, the Caughley plant was disposed of to Mr. Rose. John Rose died in 1841 and was succeeded by his nephew, who was in turn succeeded by Mr. Pugh. On the death of the latter a good deal of litigation ensued. There was no competent supervision and the firm was in danger of extinction when it was bought by C. C. Bruff (1889), who formed a limited liability company, with Mr. Gelson as manager and J. J. Bott, of Worcester, as the art director. The Swansea works were absorbed by John Rose in 1820 and a few years afterwards he purchased the Nantgarw works which had been founded by Derby workmen. A good quality of porcelain was made by Turner and he also used a rich, deep blue for printing. Rich gilding was employed and the products generally equaled those of Worcester from which it is difficult to distinguish them. Chinese subjects were also extensively used. Thomas Minton, an engraver, who afterwards founded the historic works at Stoke upon Trent, worked for Turner. At Coalport every effort was made to produce the best possible results and some really beautiful colors were realized. Considering its isolation, it is remarkable that it should have risen to the high position it did and does occupy and it is a favorable commentary on the loving care bestowed on its productions. Some of the artists who helped to establish Coalport fame are Hartshorn, landscape painter; Cook, flowers; Randall, birds, and Billingsley, who worked there until his death in 1828. It is to this factory we owe the Blue Dragon, Worm Sprig, Tournay sprig and Berlin chain patterns. During the many changes in the proprietary, the firm has always been known, as it is to-day, as John Rose & Co. Very little of the old Coalport is marked—A C. was sometimes used and also the initials C. D. and C. B. D. The present mark is a crown with the words "Coalport A. D. 1750."

The John Randall alluded to lived to be over one hundred years old. He was born September 1, 1810, and died November 16, 1910. He was also a geologist and the author of several works relating to Shropshire, the best known being "Clay Industries of Salop" and "History of Broseley." He first worked at Davenports.

MINOR CHINA WORKS.

Scattered over the country were a number of small china works. One at Pinxton, founded in 1795, found its best expression under William Billingsley, who left there in 1800, after which the body was coarser and the decorations more roughly drawn. At Church Gresley, in Leicestershire, Sir Nigel Gresley founded a china works in 1795. Good results must have been obtained as Queen Charlotte ordered "the handsomest dinner service he could make," but it was never executed potting difficulties being encountered which led to financial loss and the works were closed in 1808. At the Rockingham works china was made from about 1820 to 1842. A vase in the South Kensington Museum measures three feet two inches in height, the flower painting of which is of extraordinary fineness as to drawing and color. Dessert service, biscuit statuettes, cups and saucers, etc., were also made. The Nantgarw works, nine miles from Cardiff, were founded about 1813 by George Walker and William Billingsley, where they made a beautiful soft translucent body. It was decorated principally with birds and flowers. Vases were rarely made, the product principally consisting of plates, fancy dishes, cups and saucers, etc. The works were sold to John Rose, Coalport, in 1820, and both Walker and Billingsley went to work there. Another manufactory of china was carried on at Nantgarw after this by W. W. Young, but nothing is known of the products.

The Swansea china closely resembles that of Nantgarw and probably the formula was sold by Billingsley to Mr. L. W. Dellvyn, of the Cambrian pottery. China was only made there from 1814 to 1817. The works passed to John Rose in 1820. W. W. Young, a clever draughtsman, painted sprays of flowers, natural size with great skill and natural fidelity. Occasionally these sprays were engraved and printed and the details filled in by hand. Bisque statuettes were also made. Dellvyn gave up the manufacture of porcelain to Mr. Bevington in 1817.

A pottery at Lowestoft was started in 1756 by Hewlin Lewson to utilize the clays of the district, workmen from London being brought there. Gillingwater, in his history of Lowestoft, says the London potters, fearing competition, bribed the workmen to spoil the ware, but that notwithstanding this unhandsome treatment a further attempt was made the following year by Messrs. Walker, Brown, Alfred and Rickman, which met with no better success than the first. The culprits were, however, discovered and the factory established on a firm foundation, and in 1770 a depot in London was established. In 1775, the works were under the management of the second Robert Brown and must have attained a degree of excellence as Wedgwood was sufficiently interested to make some purchases.

The products resembled those of Chelsea and Bow, as was proved by the discovery a few years ago on the site of the works, of broken pieces and moulds from which they had been made; and it is probable that many pieces ascribed to Chelsea were made at Lowestoft. Up to 1789, the decorations were entirely in blue, when they gave way to a finer and higher class of goods. Two of the painters employed were Robert Allen and a Frenchman, named Rose. The rose is a frequent decoration, perhaps from the fact that the Tudor rose occurs in the arms of the borough. Much that we would call souvenir china was made bearing the inscription "A Trifle from Lowestoft" or "Yarmouth," as the case may be. "The paste is slightly yellowish by transmitted light, the glaze being rather bluish and not over bright. There are specks—black spots on most of the pieces while the blue is of a dull cast." The works were closed in 1803 or 1804, competition, the failure of their London agent and the destruction of a large quantity of their ware in Holland during the invasion of Napoleon rendering this action imperative.

It has been stated so often that it seems scarcely necessary to repeat that the ware of Oriental paste largely decorated with heraldic devices, initials, etc., was neither made nor decorated at Lowestoft. It probably obtained its name from the fact that Lowestoft was the port of entry. Holland at that time being the principal importer of Chinese merchandise and Lowestoft being on the Eastern coast was the most convenient port of entry from that country.

China was made at Liverpool as early as 1769 by R. Chaffers, Christian and Seth Pennington and we know that in the latter, bones formed part of the paste. It was also produced at the Herculaneum works in 1800.

HARD PORCELAIN.

China clay (Koalin) was first discovered in Cornwall, England, in 1755, by William Cookworthy, a man of good education and whose powers of observation enabled him to recognize it and to differentiate it from the fusible felspathic stone. He had been interested in the subject for some years and on making this discovery obtained a patent and founded the Plymouth works in 1768, Thomas Pitt, afterwards created Lord Camelford, furnishing the necessary capital. These works were only carried on until 1770 or 1771, when they were removed to Bristol. In 1773 Richard Champion, who had been ex-

PLYMOUTH: SALT CELLAR, WHITE SHELL WORK.

BRISTOL.

perimenting since 1765, bought Cookworthy's patent and the works were conducted by him until 1782. The Plymouth products did not reach a high degree of perfection, there was a large loss both in making and firing and the glaze was dull and thick. A French painter, named Soqui or Sequoi, was employed. Shells were freely used as motifs for salt cellars, etc., and other productions included busts, statuettes, vases and table services. The output cannot have been very considerable, but it is noteworthy as being the first works in England where true porcelain was made.

In 1772, the Bristol china was advertised as being "wholly free from the imperfections in wearing which the English china usually has and its composition as equal in fineness to the East Indian, and will wear as well. The enameled ware which is

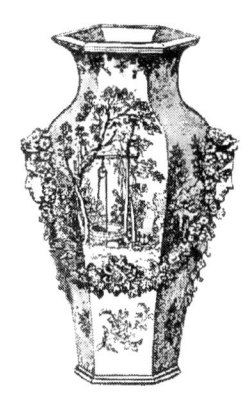

BRISTOL FIGURE.   BRISTOL HEXAGONAL VASE.

rendered nearly as cheap as the English blue and white equals the Dresden, which this work more particularly imitates." Existing specimens confirm this and show that the imitation also included the Dresden mark. The most characteristic productions of Bristol were oval or round placques with flowers and foliage in full relief, "which constitute the most marvelous triumphs of ceramic skill which has ever been produced in this style of ornament." They are much finer than the biscuit flowers made at Derby. Many beautiful figures and statuettes were made, some of which were colored and others left white. The hexagonal vase illustrated is twelve inches high, or with the cover sixteen inches, and these often had perforated necks. Occasionally they have colored or salmon scale grounds. Some very beautiful services were made for the table, the decorations were usually rich, but in good taste. The most celebrated of these was a tea set presented to Mrs. Edmund Burke. For some reason the public did not show much appreciation of the Bristol products and it never received the aristocratic patronage given to Chelsea and Worcester and it seemed impossible to make the works a pecuniary success. This led to the production of the Bristol cottage china, which commanded a ready sale. It is thin in substance and simply decorated, mostly with scattered bouquets of flowers and a border of festooned ribbons.

In 1781 Champion disposed of his patent to seven Staffordshire potters. The paste of Bristol china is of milky whiteness and of great hardness, caused by the high proportion of silica in its composition.

The purchasers of the patent continued the manufacture of porcelain at the New Hall Works, Shelton, under the style of Hollins, Warburton & Co., but the decorations were poor and clumsy, and in 1820 the body was changed, bones being introduced, and the works were closed in 1825.

CHAPTER XV.

THE MAYERS—THE WOOD FAMILY—DAVENPORT—LITTLER—LUSTERS.

Undoubtedly Wedgwood in addition to what he effected for English pottery as an art, converted it into a manufacture of commercial importance and was the first of a large number of eminent potters whose work is by no means to be overlooked. In addition to those we have mentioned there were many others, some of whom found no successors to carry on their work, whilst others have weathered the storms of time and are honored names to-day, with records extending over a century.

Elijah Mayer, Hanley, probably descended from Hugh or John Mayer, who were potters there early in the eighteenth century, made both jasper and basalte ware, the latter certainly equaling that of Wedgwood. The name is a familiar one in Staffordshire. Thomas Mayer had the Cliff Bank Works at Stoke in 1829, and three brothers, John, Thomas and Jos, succeeded Joseph Stubbs at the Dalehall Works in 1836. They introduced printing in four or five colors. The sons of Jos. Mayer came to this country and now conduct a business at Beaver Falls, Pa.

Wood is also a familiar name. The first of this name of whom we have any record was Ralph Wood of Burslem in the eighteenth century. He made a large number of groups and statuettes among which may be mentioned a bust of Washington, "The Vicar and Moses," "The Vicar and His Clerk," etc. He also made granite, or porphyry ware, made by attaching to the surface small pieces of different colored clays which were then smoothed and glazed. His son, Aaron, was apprenticed to Dr. Thomas Wedgwood, in 1731, and attained a great reputation as a block cutter and mold maker. In conjunction with William Littler he made the first blue salt glaze which resembled the finest lapis lazuli. His son, William, born in 1741, was also a skillful modeler and mold maker, and most of the useful articles made by Wedgwood at Etruria were his production. He spent his life and gave his talents to the furtherance of Wedgwood's interests, for many years at the munificent sum of £70 a year, when harassed by debts and fearful of ending his days in the poor house his pay was increased to £106 a year. His brother Enoch commenced business for himself at the old Swan Bank in Burslem, 1783, and in 1790 was joined by James Caldwell. This continued until 1818, when the firm was changed to Enoch Wood & Sons. Enoch, one of the sons, also dealt in borax and amassed a large fortune. On his withdrawal from the firm there was but little capital left, and in 1846 the other brothers went out of business. Enoch Wood, the elder, was familiarly known as "The Father of the Potteries." His busts and statuettes are well known, and many of the best of the rich deep blue American historical pieces were made by him. In addition to being a good potter he was an enthusiastic collector of Staffordshire wares, and his collection and his copious notes are the basis of much of our knowledge of early Staffordshire wares. His works were known as the Fountain Place works and were later occupied by Pinder Bourne & Co., and are now run by Messrs Doulton & Co.

Davenport will always be a name high on the roll of honor in English ceramics. John Davenport commenced business at Longport in 1794, at the works formerly occupied by John Brindley, brother of James Brindley, the famous engineer. He greatly improved the body of English china—an improvement which could not be furthered during the eighty years it was made from the same formula. He died in 1834, leaving the business to his two sons, William and Henry. The latter died in 1869, and was succeeded by his son, Henry, under whose management the works gradually decayed and were finally sold at auction.

SILVER LUSTER.
Courtesy of Keramic Studio.

RESIST LUSTER.
Courtesy of Keramic Studio.

COPPER LUSTER.
Courtesy of Keramic Studio

William Littler of Longton Hall, was making china from 1752 to 1758, but how much longer we do not know. The body was similar to that of the early Chelsea and did not contain bone. A very rich blue streaked and run is a characteristic of this china, and plates and dishes with vine-leaf decorations. William Duesbury, afterwards of Derby, was connected with the Longton Hall Works. The mark was a cross L. with three dots underneath. Specimens of this china are quite rare.

According to Jewitt, John Hancock first used lusters when working for Spode some time after 1769, the date of his apprenticeship. At the beginning of the nineteenth century they were made by nearly every manufacturer in Staffordshire. Sometimes the whole surface of the piece inside and out was covered with a thin coating of silver and when the Georgian models of the silversmiths were used, the pieces closely resembled genuine silverware—or a design of leaves and flowers was applied in a preparation not affected by the silver and the remainder covered with that metal. This gave the effect of a white pattern on a silver ground and such pieces are known as "resist luster." The copper was also applied on a solid ground, but more often with bands, ovals, etc., either white or colored, on which patterns were printed or roughly painted, or embossed designs highly colored were introduced. This manufacture assumed considerable importance and though generally abandoned has never entirely ceased, such firms as Charles Allerton & Sons having continuously produced it. For a time the secret of the silver luster seems to have been lost, or perhaps it would be more correct to say that no effort was made by those who could do so to resurrect it, but the demand having arisen it has been filled and now silver lusters are again a commercial article. Any amateur with a decorating kiln can very easily produce these lusters, which are sold by all potters' supply houses. Of course, the changes were rung on these two metals and we have pink and purple lusters, etc., which by no means equaled in appearance the silver and copper. Luster ware was also made at Sunderland, Leeds and other places.

CHAPTER XVI.

MINTON—DOULTON—CAULDON.

Thomas Minton, the founder of the firm of Mintons, was born at Wyle Cop, Shrewsbury, in 1766, and was apprenticed to Thomas Turner, of the Caughley China Works, as an engraver.

A POTTERY PRIMER. 117

Here, it has been stated, he engraved the famous Willow pattern, but the original Caughley engraving bears the initials of Turner. He later went to London, and soon after his marriage, in 1789, he removed to Stoke, and from an engraver became a potter, building a small works on the site of the present manufactory, somewhere about 1793 to 1796. He had as a partner Joseph Poulson, a practical potter, and the combination proved a good one. Minton & Poulson was the style of the firm. When William Pownall, who had rendered them financial assistance, entered the firm it was changed to Minton, Poulson & Pownall. The products consisted almost entirely of printed earthenware. In 1817, Messrs. Poulson & Pownall having retired, Thomas Minton's sons, Thomas Webb and Herbert, were admitted to partnership, the former retiring in 1821. Herbert at a very early age showed remarkable ability, and when Thomas Minton died in 1836, he became sole proprietor, admitting to partnership soon afterwards, John Boyle, and the style of the firm was changed from Thomas Minton & Sons to Minton & Boyle. This partnership lasted five years, when Mr. Boyle became a partner with Wedgwood. In 1845 Mr. Michael Daintry Hollins, nephew of Mrs. Minton, was admitted to the firm, and in the year following Mr. Colin Minton Campbell, Herbert Minton's nephew and heir. Herbert Minton died in 1858, and the business was continued by the remaining partners until 1867, when it was dissolved, Mr. Hollins continuing the manufacture of tiles under the style of Minton, Hollins & Co., and Mr. Campbell the remainder of the business. There was considerable litigation as to the right to use the name Minton on tiles, and the highest court upholding Mr. Hollins, the firm of R. Minton, Taylor & Co., which was really a branch of the firm of Minton & Co., was enjoined from using their name. Mr. Campbell then started The Campbell Tile Co., and the firm still continues the manufacture of encaustic tiles, Mr. John Campbell being at the head of it. After the dissolution Mr. C. M. Campbell admitted his two nephews, Thomas

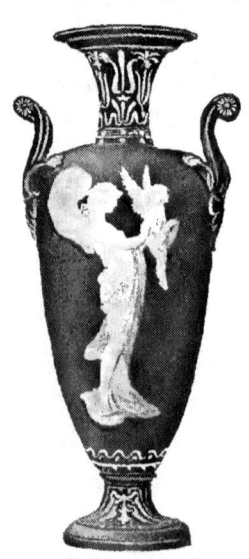

VASE BY SOLON.

and Herbert Minton, into partnership, and the name was changed from H. Minton & Co. to Minton & Co. When Mr. Campbell died in 1883, the business was transformed into a limited liability company under the present style of Mintons, Limited.

At the beginning of the eighteenth century the Minton works gave employment to about fifty hands, and this number had risen to fifteen hundred at the time of Herbert Minton's death. Herbert Minton was a great organizer as well as a good potter and had unbounded faith as to the possibilities of pottery. Neither the manufacture of encaustic tiles nor porcelain buttons were his initiative, but he had acumen enough to know their importance and the courage to use his capital to demonstrate it. He much extended the range of colors made by potters of the Middle Ages, and Minton tiles became known the world over.

As far back as 1798 an attempt had been made to make china, and was continued with no great success until 1811, when it was abandoned. It was, however, resumed in 1821, and has been manufactured continuously to the present day, the beauty of the paste and glaze, the exquisite colors realized on it and the care in its finish making it a standard of excellence which has made Minton china a household word. The earlier patterns were strongly reminiscent of Derby, and when that factory began to decline many of the workmen joined the Minton works, and the decorations rapidly improved. Bancroft, Steel and Hancock were the principal fruit and flower painters. John Simpson was the principal figure painter from 1837 to 1847, and Samuel Bourne, who served his apprenticeship to Wood & Caldwall, was designer-in-chief.

In 1849 Mr. Minton was fortunate enough to secure the services of Leon Arnoux, the son of a potter of Apt, France, and whatever triumphs were achieved by the house of Minton from the time he entered it are so inseparably connected with his skill as a potter and his wonderfully developed artistic taste as to make the recitals of one but the triumphs of the other. No ceramic puzzle seemed too difficult for him to solve, and he occupies in English the same position as the illustrious Brongniart does in French ceramics. In 1892 he retired for a few years, but an upheaval in the management of the company occurring his services were again requisitioned, and he devoted his energies to the establishment until shortly before his death in 1902.

In no single establishment has there been gathered together such a galaxy of talent as in the Minton firm. Emile Jeannest, a sculptor of refined taste, Carrière-Belleuse and M. Protat, who was working for the firm as late as 1858, followed each other, and their beautiful creations added luster and dignity to the productions of the firm. One of Mr. Arnoux's first achievements was the manufacture of hard porcelain for laboratory purposes, said to equal that of Meissen, but the difficulty of making saggers capable of standing the high heat caused the abandonment of the manufacture.

Parian was made almost concurrently with the Copeland production in 1845 or 1846.

When Herbert Minton died he left worthy successors behind him, Mr. Hollins devoting most of his interest to the tile business and Mr. Campbell to the remaining branches. While the latter had but little knowledge as a potter, he was a man of good taste, quick to perceive the trend of public taste, and loyally backed Mr. Arnoux utterly regardless of expense. After the Franco-Prussian War the artistic staff, already very large, was greatly increased, some of those who became associated with the firm being A. Boullemier, a painter of cupids and figures with remarkable technique; M. Mussill, probably the best underglaze bird and flower painter the ceramic world has ever seen, and L. Solon, whose charming creations in pâte-sur-pâte are the finest examples of this process ever produced. It required some courage to add these three to an artistic force which already comprised such men as Thomas Allen, who was later art director for Wedgwoods; Richard W. Pilsbury, whose refined flower painting ranked him as an artist of the first class. Mr. Jahn, Mr. Henk, Mr. Eyre and Mr. Wise, all good figure painters; T. Simpson, flowers, and Charles Toft, whose reproductions of the famous *faïence d' Oiron* and other no less difficult ceramic productions rank him as the first craftsman of his day (died 1883). In addition to this formidable list of painters, Coleman was furnishing designs for nature services; Dr. Dresser for border patterns, and Moyer Smith for tiles. The modeling force was equally large in proportion, and the expense must have been enormous. The greatest variety of goods is produced, practically everything that comes under the meaning of ceramics, if we except building bricks and the very cheap ware for domestic purposes.

DOULTONS.

The process of evolution, the endowment of an artistic expression to a common material; the possibilities of the fictile art when brains take the place of precedent and originality succeeds imitation, are all exemplified in the Doulton stoneware. Established in 1818 by John Doulton and John Watts in Vauxhall Walk, Lambeth, the production consisted mainly of stoneware bottles. The year of the Reform bill, 1832, gave a great impetus to this trade and thousands of flat bottles, the neck representing the King, Lord Gray, John Russell and Broughton, were made, John Doulton, who was an expert thrower, often making two hundred two-gallon bottles a day.

Henry Doulton, his son, succeeded to the business in 1846. Drain pipes and stoneware sinks were then the staple production and to meet the demand works were established at St. Helens, Rowley Regis and Smethwick. To Henry Doulton must be given the credit of having constructed the first potter's wheel driven by steam, and it was ten years later before there was another in use either in London or Staffordshire. Henry Doulton was a man of artistic temperament and he had long recognized the artistic possibilities of the stoneware he made, but it was not until 1870 that he commenced to carry out his ideas in this direction. There was no imitation of an antique type; all was distinctly creative and all that was artistic found encouragement. The decorations were incised with a blunt tool, afterward colored with a brush and a salt glaze applied. Neither the incising nor the use of salt glaze was an original process, and yet with these two old methods Doulton constructed a distinct type "sober, quiet, harmonious and deep, full of quality." The trio who first gave artistic grace to this Doulton stoneware were Mrs. Hannah B. Barlow, Miss Florence E. Barlow and Mrs. Frank A. Butler, the latter a deaf mute. Not satisfied with the success achieved, Mr. Doulton, after some experimenting, evolved "Silicon" ware, which is a stoneware without a salt glaze, the effects being produced by various colored clays. This was followed in 1888 by Carrara ware, a stoneware similar in texture to marble, the surface being of an eggshell texture. "Crown Lambeth" was introduced in 1891. "Lambeth faience" has the decorations in colors painted under the glaze. Miss F. Lewis and M. V. Marshall having produced many noteworthy pieces. In "Vitreous fresco" A. E. Pearce and J. Eyre have done fine work.

The name of George Tinworth is almost as familiar with the Doulton works as that of Doulton himself. He commenced working in the pottery in 1867, retouching old molds, but it was not long before he launched into more original work, modeling filters and making enlarged copies of old molds, some of these attracting the attention of the eminent art critic, John Ruskin. While he had a fund of humor that found expression in some of his works, it is his religious subjects that gave him his deserved fame. Their excellence in thought, composition and modeling attracted universal attention, and while the story is always simply told, it is told with a virile strength that appeals to the least appreciative. They have not been inaptly called "The Bible in Sculpture." In the Smithsonian Institute at Washington is a Doulton pulpit with panels by Tinworth illustrating scenes in the life of the Christ from the offering in the Temple to the Ascension.

Henry Doulton, for his services to the ceramic art, was knighted in 1887, a distinction never before or since bestowed on an English potter. He was created a Chevalier of the Legion of Honor in 1878, and in the course of his life received no less than 105 diplomas of honor, 110 gold and 102 silver medals. He died November 18, 1897, and during his sixty years of service had watched his works steadily grow from the time when a blind horse was the only motive power used until it needed 3,500 horse-power to keep the wheels of the great Lambeth factory moving.

In 1877 the firm entered into partnership with T. Shadford Pinder, for the purpose of making fine china and earthenware, but this partnership was dissolved in 1881, Mr. Pinder retiring and the firm name was changed to Doulton & Co. Mr. Bailey was appointed manager, a position he continues to hold. Their most noteworthy productions are the Sang de Boeuf of Mr. Bernard Moore and some really exquisite effects in crystalline glazes.

CAULDON.

For 150 years the name of Ridgway has been inseparably connected with English pottery. While Job Ridgway was the first of that name to attain any distinction we know that he came of a family of potters, for on the death of his mother in 1765, he being seven years of age at the time, his father and an elder brother went to Swansea to positions in the newly established pottery there. Here he was apprenticed, but returned to the Potteries in 1780. Failing to find work he drifted to Leeds, again returning to Hanley in 1782, and two years later married the sister of Elijah Mayer. In due course three sons were born to them, John, William and Joseph, the latter dying when only nine months old. Soon after his marriage he entered into partnership with his brother George as manufacturers of earthenware, and the venture must have been successful, for when this partnership was amicably dissolved he built the Cauldon Works, where he established a business known for many years as Job Ridgway & Sons. He made earthenware and stoneware, and a little later blue-printed ware. While the manufacture did not assume much importance, the wares were favorably known, but it was not until it came under the management of his sons, John and William, that the leading manufacturers discovered that they had in them formidable rivals.

About 1802 Job Ridgway tried to revive the old Hull Pottery, and did considerably extend the trade, but he sold out his interests in 1804 to Messrs. Smith, his partners. What the arrangements was we do not know, but two years later the Smiths assigned all their interests to Job and George Ridgway, who carried on the works until 1826, though Job died in 1814. To John Ridgway's skill as a potter and to his untiring energy is largely due the success of the Cauldon Works. Soon after 1815 he introduced a bone china body and added to it a rich and luscious glaze, making the applied color extremely fine in tone. In 1822 he visited the United States, and a large trade with them was established. The English potter was then catering largely to this market, and what is known as American historical pottery was sold in large quantities. This consisted chiefly of printed services in a very deep and rich blue, with portraits of her heroes or statesmen and scenery. Of such a character was the Beauties of America service issued by Ridgway and which must have had an immense sale. Shortly after his return from America the partnership between himself and his brother, William, was dissolved. About this time, too, there was a noticeable improvement in the shapes and the productions had been so improved as to command the attention of royalty, and Queen Victoria authorized the use of the sub-title, "Potter to Her Majesty." Since that time the Cauldon Works has continuously received royal patronage, both from Windsor and Osborne. In 1859 John Ridgway retired, the business passing to T. C. Brown-Westhead, Mr. Bates and William Moore, who had learned practical pottery under John Ridgway. The name of the firm became and continues to be T. C. Brown-Westhead, Moore & Co., though for the sake of brevity the products are known as Cauldon. On the death of William Moore, in 1866, his brother, James, took his place, was admitted as a partner in 1875 and died in 1881. Mr. Brown-Westhead died in 1882, and the business passed into the hands of W. B. & F. T. Moore, sons of William Moore. Later the business was turned into a limited company.

The Cauldon productions are extremely various, and a very high standard is maintained throughout. The Cauldon china is especially noticeable, and in purity of body, in manufacturing skill and general excellence is certainly not excelled by any other make. The various international exhibitions where Cauldon goods are always a conspicous feature have sealed their product with their approval; an approval which was only their just due, and the mark has long been an index as a guarantee of excellence. At the Brussels Exhibitition the company received a Grand Prix for its fine show of china, which later was lost in the great fire.

CHAPTER XVIII.

RIDGWAYS—COBRIDGE WORKS—BELLEEK—BOOTE—MASON—JONES—WEDGWOOD & CO.—BOOTHS—MINOR POTTERIES.

RIDGWAYS.

The early history of this house has been given in our sketch of the Cauldon Works. When William Ridgway separated from his brother, about 1830, he rented the Church Street works, Hanley, from Joseph Mayer, and eventually became the proprietor of no less than six manufactories, among which were the Bell Works, now Clemenson Brothers and the one now occupied by

RIDGWAY STONEWARE JUGS.

Geo. L. Ashworth & Brothers. His trade with America was greatly increased by a visit here, and Charles Cartledge, afterwards a manufacturer at Greenpoint, acted as his agent. He also commenced the erection of a manufactory in Kentucky, but it was never completed, his affairs becoming involved.

His son, Edward John, was admitted into partnership and

the business was carried on by them until William Ridgway's death in 1864. The former then entered into partnership with L. J. Abington under the style of Ridgway and Abington. This partnership was dissolved in 1866, and E. J. Ridgway built the Bedford Works at Shelton. Mr. Sparks, the firm's London agent, and Mr. Ridgway's two sons, John and E. A., were admitted into partnership in 1872, and the firm name was Ridgway, Sparks & Ridgway, E. J. Ridgway retiring. He died in 1896. Upon the death of Mr. Sparks, in 1878, the name was changed to Ridgways. The products consist mostly of earthenware and stoneware, both of excellent quality.

Of the former it is sufficient criterion to say that several of the dinnerware patterns have been of late years reissued, meeting with great success, the beautiful engraving being a noteworthy feature. The same remark may be applied to the stoneware jugs, which are artistically conceived and well modeled, the originals dating from 1834. These reissues are valuable, as they tend to show the excellence of manufacture the firm had attained seventy-five years ago; an excellence they are jealous to maintain.

THE COBRIDGE WORKS.

Cobridge lies midway between Hanley and Burslem. Works were erected there in 1808 by Bucknall & Stevenson, who were succeeded by A. Stevenson. In 1816 to 1820 they passed into the hands of James Clews, and he continued them until 1829. The works remained closed until 1836, when they were reopened by Robinson, Wood & Brownfield, Brownfield being the sole surviving partner in 1850. In 1871 his son, W. E. Brownfield, was admitted as a partner, and the firm name became W. Brownfield & Sons. W. Brownfield died in 1873, and shortly after it was, in the interests of the work people converted into a co-operative company, known as the Brownfield Guild Pottery. The most interesting phase of this old pottery was the occupancy by James Clews, who issued a large number of American historical subjects printed in a deep blue, the best known of which are "The Landing of Lafayette," and the States series. Clews came to this country in 1837 and built a factory at Troy, Ind., but even with the assistance of the English potters brought here it was a dismal failure and he returned to England. One son remained here, the financier, Henry Clews. James Carr, the veteran New York potter, worked for Clews and afterwards employed many of the potters from the Troy factory.

The best period of the Brownfield pottery was between 1870 and 1880, when, under the directorship of Mr. Jahn, an artist of ability, the productions were considerably improved and successfully competed with the more well-known firms of the district.

When the Guild pottery was instituted F. A. Rhead, who had had his training at Mintons and Wedgwoods, and later served as art director for Bodleys, was the art director, but the cumbrous committee of workingmen who constituted the management failed to understand his artistic instincts, and what had been conceived by Mr. Brownfield for the good and betterment of all concerned ended in disastrous failure. Dressed in a little brief authority, each shareholding workman considered himself an absolute dictator. There was much ludicrous quarreling, and the whole proceedings rivaled the merriest *opera bouffe*.

BELLEEK.

The product known as Belleek is a fine parian body washed with metallic lusters. These pearly lusters were the invention of J. J. H. Brianchou, who protected by patent his discovery in France, England and Germany. They were used both in France and Germany, and coming to the notice of W. H. Goss, of Stoke, about 1863, he experimented with them. In the same year McBirney & Armstrong, of the Belleek Works, engaged Goss' foreman, William Bromley, a modeler named Gallimore and several workmen from the same factory to develop the same idea. The manufacture was extensively carried on and became popular, a good deal of encouraged misapprehension existing as to the means of production. The lusters were simply imported from the patentee, a wash of them applied to glazed parian and fired at a low heat. Bromley came to America in 1883 to assist J. Hart Brewer in his development of Belleek. The W. H. Goss alluded to started in business at Stoke in 1858 as a manufacturer of parian, and soon turned his attention to small pieces with college badges and similar heraldic devices, building up an extensive trade and creating a style which is still popular. The daintiness, good potting and restraint in decoration are some of the factors that insured this success.

The works occupied by T. & R. Boote were founded at the end of the eighteenth century by Walter Daniel, who was succeeded by Timothy and John Lockett. In 1809 Joseph Machin and Jacob Baggaley were the proprietors, the former giving place to William Machin in 1831. Later they were succeeded by Richard Daniel and Thomas Edwards, and in 1850 the works passed into the hands of the present proprietors. They were among the early manufacturers of parian, but abandoned it so as to devote their energies more particularly to staple productions in a semi-porcelain body. About five years ago they discontinued the manufacture of earthenware and devoted all their energies to the extension and improvement of tiles, of which they are very large producers.

MASON'S IRONSTONE CHINA.

Charles James Mason, of Fenton, in 1813, took out a patent for the manufacture of ironstone china, powdered iron slag being one of its constituent parts. The body was of extreme hardness and purity of color. For want of capital Mason was obliged to sell his business and the patent in 1851 to Francis Morley, who continued its manufacture, and was awarded a first-class medal in the French exhibition of 1856. Morley, some sixteen or seventeen years ago, sold his entire business to Geo. L. Ashworth & Bros., who continue the manufacture of ironstone china at their works at Shelton. The peculiar nature of the body adapts it to very rich colorings, and the red and blue Japan patterns, both of the old Mason and the product of to-day, are very brilliant and effective. Morley was succeeded at Fenton by Baker & Co.

Josiah Spode, born in 1773, died in 1797, was an apprentice of Whieldons and he commenced business on his own account in 1770 at the works at Stoke formerly occupied by Banks & Turner. His son learned the business from him and together with his traveler, William Copeland, they conducted the business so efficiently as to at once make a mark. The first products were earthenware, the designs largely drawn from Oriental sources, but in 1800 they commenced to make china. It is often stated that Spode was the first to use bone in its composition but we have already seen that long before it had been utilized at Chelsea, Bow, etc. In 1805 he introduced a fine and durable body which he called Stone China of which Queen Charlotte bought a service. Josiah

JOSIAH SPODE.

Spode, 2d, died in 1827 and Copeland in 1826. The son of the latter, W. T. Copeland, bought the business from Josiah Spode, 3d, in 1833, and taking into partnership his traveler, Thomas Garrett, from 1833 to 1847, the title of the firm was Copeland & Garrett. Upon the dissolution of this partnership the name was changed to W. T. Copeland late Spode. Then Alderman Copeland (he was once Lord Mayor of London) took into partnership his four sons and the present style of W. T. Copeland & Sons was adopted. The only surviving member of the firm is Richard Pirie Copeland. It was the first firm to make parian. The Spodes undoubtedly added much to the prestige of English pottery, their productions being highly esteemed and are regarded by connoisseurs as the best expression of the potters' art of that period. During the administration of Mr. F. R. Abraham (up to 1896) some excellent work was produced, assisted as he was by such able artists as Hürten (flowers); Besche, Alcock, Hewitt and Abraham (figures) and Yale (landscapes).

Wileman & Co., Longton. Mr. Percy Shelley, B. A., has raised this pottery to one of the first rank, elevating its products from a cheap grade of earthenware to a fine china and a line of ornamental earthenware of an artistic if somewhat severe character, mostly painted under the glaze.

Furnivals, Ltd., Cobridge. Thomas Furnival & Co. succeeded Reuben Johnson & Co. at the Stafford Street Works, Hanley, the name being shortly afterwards changed to Furnival & Clark and so remained until 1851 when the present works at Cobridge were taken and the style of the firm became Thomas Furnival & Sons, afterwards changed to Furnivals, Limited. Their productions have been almost entirely confined to staple goods and are characterized by careful potting and excellence of designs. Especially is this true of their toilet services, which are marked by originality and beauty of design and which have never been approached by their larger competitors. Mr. W. M. Binns, formerly of Worcester, is now associated with them and has just produced a line of flower holders, bowls and other utilitarian articles with exquisite crystalline glazes, which we have pleasure to illustrate, for they ought readily to take the place of the meritricious pieces usually sold for such purposes. They term this artistic and beautiful ware "Maniora faïence."

Hammersley & Co., Longton, are manufacturers of bone china, one of the few houses in Longton producing china dinner ware which may be considered as the supreme test of the potters' skill. The body is a good one and the decorations are in good taste, comparing favorably in both respects with the products of more well known houses.

Redfern & Drakeford, Normacott, have in their excellent china dinner ware gone for inspiration to the successes of some of the old potters and have brought out some fine designs in the style of Crown, Derby and Swansea, as well as elaborate incrustations and other richly designed effects.

Williamson & Son, Longton, adopt greater originality in design than many houses and have had several distinct successes, among which their Gainsboro designs adapted from cretonnes are

MAMORA FAIENCE.

noticeable. This class of design makes it possible for the china to match the draperies of a room and is especially attractive for breakfast rooms. Another service is decorated with Blue Birds, let us hope "for Happiness."

These and other houses have done much to raise the standard of Longton china, so that the term is no longer indicative of mere cheapness, and it is only a matter of time if the present advance in quality and style is maintained, before they leave some of their old time competitors in the rear.

The Crown Sutherland Works, Hanley, under the guidance of Mr. A. Leger, produce much elaborately gilt china dinner ware. Mr. Leger learned his art in France, adapting it to English ideas at Mintons and Cauldon, where he did much fine work, and now that he has a business of his own he is demonstrating the ease with which French taste and English workmanship can be combined and how happy a result can be realized.

George Jones & Sons, Stoke-upon-Trent. Established by George Jones, with the assistance of E. B. Jackson, of Manchester, as a whiteware factory at the Old Bridge Works in 1861. To meet trade demands the Trent works were built, and china, earthenware and majolica were made. George Jones died in 1893. His son, Frank, later known as Frank Jones-Benham, became an expert potter, and much of the success that has attended their efforts is due to his skill. Another son, Horace, a clever artist, is responsible for much of the decoration. The quality of the gilding on the Jones china has always been noticeable, and while never over-burdened to the point of vulgarity, it has a solidity and quality which imparts a certain elegance to it. The trade mark is a crescent and the monogram of the firm.

S. Alcock & Co. were established at the Hill Top Pottery, Burslem, in 1839, the works having previously been occupied by Ralph Wood. In 1866 they passed into the hands of the Hill Top Pottery Co., which liquidated in 1867. Part of the works was taken by Alcock & Diggory, who were succeeded by Bodley and Diggory, 1870; E. F. Bodley, 1871; Bodley & Son, 1875, and finally E. J. D. Bodley. Bodley made a beautiful china body, one which has probably never been surpassed. E. F. Bodley supplied the service for the Confederate steamer Alabama.

Ralph Wedgwood, a second cousin of Josiah Wedgwood, was born in 1766, and served his apprenticeship as a potter at Etruria. In 1796 he joined the firm of Tomlinson & Co., Ferrybridge, Yorkshire, the new firm adopting the title of Wedgwood & Co. This partnership only lasted until about the end of the century, when Ralph Wedgwood retired. He is said to have been in business at the Hill Top Works, Burslem, that the war with America caused his failure there and furnished the reason for his migration to Yorkshire.

The present firm of Wedgwood & Co., Tunstall, was founded in 1830, was incorporated as a bonded liability company in 1900, the style of the firm being then changed to Wedgwood & Co., Ltd. Some interesting historical pieces were issued by them, usually printed in black, a jug with portraits of Washington and Franklin being a good example. Another early design had classical figure subjects in the center and in compartments in the border, both engraving and printing being finely executed. Like many other Staffordshire potters, they have been satisfied not to invade the realms of ornamental pottery, devoting all their attention to the improvement of their utilitarian wares, and with implicit confidence in the merit of their "Imperial Porcelain," have lavished on it high-grade decorations usually reserved for porcelain, and the result has happily justified their faith. Some of the decorations, especially those where mazarine blue is a dominant note, are triumphs of the decorator's skill, the beautiful glaze bringing out the colors to the best advantage. They also make a specialty of blue willow and other blue-prints. There has never been any inclination to trade on the reputation of their namesakes, the trade mark being quite distinctive: (1) In 1870 a unicorn's head and Wedgwood & Co. on a ribbon; (2) 1890, lion surmounting a crown; (3) 1910, on high-grade goods, a crown and their name.

BOOTHS, LTD., TUNSTALL.

This is an old firm of earthenware manufacturers, which has been in existence since 1830. The original firm was Evans & Booth, occupying the Knowles Works. In 1868 the style was changed to Thos. Booth & Co., in 1872 to T. G. & F. Booth, and is now conducted by the former alone, under the style of Booths, Ltd. In 1870 they moved to the Church Bank Works, which they now occupy. During recent years the productions have changed for the better very largely, the body has been improved to its present standard, and the house may be regarded as one of the most progressive in the Potteries. They have been particularly successful with decoration in which a rich cobalt is the dominant color. They were awarded a medal at St. Louis in 1864. The series of English scenes from old Davenport copper plates, applied to beakers, vases, dessert and dinner ware are worthy of mention.

John Aynsley & Sons, Longton, were established in the first part of last century. They make a good quality of bone china, and there are several other firms of the name of Aynsley in Longton. John Aynsley was a working potter and made a large fortune, being financially interested in many of the Longton potteries whose necessities his capital enabled him to take advantage of.

Harvey Adams & Co., Longton, china, founded in 1862, where Henry Mitchell, an animal and landscape painter did some of his best work.

A POTTERY PRIMER. 131

Moore Bros., Longton, china. An extremely good body, used principally for figure subjects, often in combination with the lotus leaves and flowers; finished in silver and gold of rich quality and always judiciously applied. Some good examples of Pâte-sur-pâte were also produced. Mr. Bernard Moore, the senior partner, for years devoted himself to the solving of the problem of fine red glazes of the Chinese, and finally succeeded, transferring their production to Messrs. Doulton & Co., Burslem. Mr. Moore's scientific research, or its result, has been freely communicated to the potters of the district, much to their benefit.

C. MEIGH JUGS.
Courtesy of Keramic Studio.

The old Hall Earthenware Co., Hanley, started by Job Meigh, in 1790, was succeeded by Chas. Meigh & Son, and some time after 1851 was incorporated. The Meighs were both clever potters, and their stoneware, jugs, etc., are deservedly esteemed by collectors. The company was dissolved in 1902.

CHAPTER XVIII.
FOR THE AMERICAN MARKET.

The potter who gives us our services for the table and imbues the things of daily use with an artistic expression is perhaps more entitled to our thanks than the manufacturer who furnishes, sometimes very useless ornaments, exclusively for the wealthy.

John Maddock, the founder of the house of John Maddock & Sons, commenced business in 1830. Shortly afterward seeing the great possibilities of trade with this country he sent his son, John Maddock, Jr., to study the wants and conditions of the market, the result of which was reaped by his brothers, Thomas and Henry, who succeeded him. Another brother, James Maddock, is now the head of the house, and is the only surviving son. Upon the death of John Maddock, Jr., his son, John Francis, was admitted by his uncle as a partner. From its inception there has been but one ambition, and every energy has been bent to the one end, to attain that degree of excellence that the ware produced by the firm should constitute a standard of value which no competitor must be allowed to excel. In the early period white ware only was made, but when the Philadelphia exhibition taught us the crudity with which we had been satisfied and instigated the desire for an enrichment of our table services, the Maddock firm was quick to respond to the demand, and skilled engravers were employed to make designs, and some beautiful printed patterns were the result. The careful manner in which these designs were transferred and printed soon made them popular, and while the firm has of late years used decalcomania very extensively, it still maintains its reputation for printed ware, and there are not lacking signs that the day of the engraver and printer may return.

Alfred Meakin bought the works formerly occupied by Turner & Tompkinson, Tunstall, in 1881. He died in 1902.

James Meakin commenced business in Longton in 1845 and moved to Hanley in 1848. He retired in 1852 and was succeeded by his sons James and George, who in 1859 built the Eagle Works at Joiners Square. They have branch works at Cobridge and Burslem, and the firm is one of the largest in the district. James Meakin died in 1885 and George in 1891. In 1890 the business was converted into a limited liability company, of which George E. Meakin is chairman. The Meakins have always been something more than large employers of labor, they have been public spirited men, who have freely spent their money for the benefit of the worker, and Staffordshire is indebted to them for many excellent institutions.

Johnson Brothers, Hanley, occupy the historic Charles Street Works, founded by William Mellor in 1758. He made Egyptian black ware, as did his successors, Toft & Wheeling. Toft & May succeeded them, and a little later May conducted the business alone. He was succeeded by William Ridgway, but the business—white ware for the American market—did not prove a success, and J. W. Pankhurst & Co. next occupied them. On Mr. Pankhurst's death, some 25 years ago, they passed into the hands of their present proprietors, Johnson Brothers, and almost immediately assumed importance.

Other manufacturers who specially cater to the American market are W. H. Grindley & Co., Tunstall; Wood & Son, Burslem; Mellor, Taylor & Co., Tunstall, 1880, both graduates of the Meakin Works; A. J. Wilkinson & Co., Burslem; Bourne & Leigh, who succeeded Blackhurst & Bourne; Edward Challinor (Baker & Co.), who succeeded Bourne, Baker & Bourne, one of the first firms to introduce printing in the potteries, and Henry Alcock & Co., Cobridge.

Another class consists of those firms who have come into existence in recent years, whose products are known in this market, and a few details concerning them may be of interest and possibly—in some cases, probably—furnish data to some future historian.

Gater, Hall & Co., Burslem, originally founded by T. & J. A. Hall in 1892. Earthenware, principally jugs and toilet sets.

Sandlands, Ltd., Hanley—W. Sandland was in business at Stoke from 1883 to 1893, making a cheap grade of earthenware. In the latter year he removed to Hanley, and added the manufacture of bone china. They also make a line of vases, the decoration of which is principally mechanical.

A. G. Harley Jones, Fenton, founded in 1901. The products consist of ornamental goods, the best work being painted in underglaze colors. Photographs by an ingenious method are reproduced on the ware and afterward colored. The art department is under the direction of Mr. Warsop. Mr. Jones is a trained potter and has succeeded in building up a large business.

E. Brain & Co., Fenton, established 1850. Manufacture bone china in modern art designs of a very choice quality. The ware is known as Foley art china, and more particularly as Peacock china, an honor paid to the designer, Mr. Peacock, who has produced a series of patterns with somewhat of an Art Nouveau feeling, but without the extravagance of that school, being very simple in design and quiet and restful in coloring. The usual gold adornment has been dispensed with, and would in fact be out of place, the quality of body and decoration being deemed sufficient to hold attention. Mr. Elijah Brain, the founder, died October, 1910.

The Soho Pottery Co., Tunstall, earthenware, was established in 1860 and remodeled in 1904. Mr. S. J. Simpson is the managing director.

Alfred Colley & Co., Tunstall, earthenware, dinner and tea

ware, established 1909, from the style and quality of their initial productions promise to be prominently heard from in the future. Alfred Colley, the managing director, for twenty-five years held a responsible position with Johnson Brothers. The mark is a crown with the name of the firm.

MacIntyre & Co., Burslem, manufacturers of door furniture, etc., considerably increased their reputation with a line of ornamental goods, which they call Florian. The design is drawn on the ware in a raised line by means of a small glass tube inserted in a rubber ball filled with slip and the pattern then painted with colored clays. The method is an improvement on an old one, but the result is so charming it was accepted as something

ART CHINA, BY E. BRAIN & CO., FENTON, ENG.

quite new, which indeed it was. The coloring at first was subdued, consisting mostly of grays and blues; the designs are good and the finish beyond reproach. In the hands of Mr. W. Moorcroft, who is responsible for most of the designs, Florian ware has undergone many changes, and whilst maintaining its original character and beauty the present day production varies considerably from that of ten years ago, being distinguished by a warmth of coloring rendered very unobstrusive by the hard fire it is subject to. This ware is an exemplification of how artistic pottery can be produced at a moderate price, pure in shape and the decoration conforming in every particular to the laws that should, but seldom do, govern it. (See illustration, page 158.)

CHAPTER XIX.

ENGLISH ARTIST POTTERS—POTTERIES OUTSIDE STAFFORDSHIRE

It is a rather serious reflection that not only in England, but in France, Germany and the United States, the most meritorious by amateurs. In England the names of De Morgan and Howson Taylor; in France, Lachenal, Deck and Carrière; in Germany, Schmutz-Baudiss, and in America, Mrs. Bellamy Storer. In England, in which we are now interested, "the manufacturers and even the scientists," to quote Mr. F. A. Rhead, "look on mat and crystalline glazes as a phase, interesting if somewhat freaky, and not by any means as the Ultima Thule of Ceramic Art." As an instance of this, the Worcester Co. have exhibited some fine specimens of crystalline glazes but, we believe, have never placed them on the market, and yet it will be readily owned that this is a greater ceramic achievement than gilding on raised paste.

William De Morgan was a stained glass painter, yet he gave to England perhaps the most artistic pottery ever made there and rediscovered the iridescent lusters of the Italian potters of the sixteenth century. His ingenuity suggested a method in producing the designs never before attempted and which proved perfectly satisfactory. Associated with him at various times were such men as William Morris and Halsey Ricardo and a number of clever Italian craftsmen. The work commenced in 1869 and has continued to grow in favor, many steamship lines using De Morgan's tiles for interior decorations. It is no small matter that the same man should have given to the world these wonderful specimens of ceramics and have contributed to literature works of fiction which place him among the foremost writers of the day.

MARTIN STONEWARE.

Harold Rathbone started the Della Robbia Pottery at Birkenhead, about twenty-five years ago, the product, as the name suggests, being based on Italian models. With the assistance of such men as the late Ford Maddox-Brown and Conrad Dressler, some most interesting pottery was produced, and it is much to be regretted that either through lack of proper management or some similar cause, the venture was discontinued in 1901.

The Martin Brothers commenced making the fine salt glaze stoneware which bears their name, at Fulham in 1872, and seven years later they built a kiln at Southall. The decorations are carved, engraved or modeled on the pieces, but then is their harmony of color, which impresses one with a sense of absolute satisfaction. The work is practically all done by the four brothers, the most gifted one being R. W. Martin, who, when a student at the Royal Academy, "did work which marked him out as one who would even in England, where sculpture does not hold a favored place, in time achieve renown." It was fortunate for lovers of ceramics that Mr. Martin preferred to express his fancies in an art which appeals to a wider circle rather than confine it to marble. The productions of the firm have done much to emphasize how beautiful stoneware may become in the hands of such competent artist-craftsmen.

Dr. Mellor is producing some extraordinary crystalline glazes, being apparently able to regulate their size and character and more than that, their position on the piece. Howson Taylor, the maker of Ruskin ware, seems to have a similar command over mat glazes, some of the colors realized being most remarkable and, while seeming to glow, are yet as soft as a gray. He is a fine artist, rarely uses any decoration on his pottery, and when he does so it is of the simplest character, so simple and restrained and so much in place that you feel it is the one thing needful.

The Staffordshire tile manufacturers, especially Minton Hollins & Co., have all good mat glazes, as have also Maw & Co., of Broseley, and Pilkington, of Manchester. Thanks to the services of Mr. William Burton, and the collaboration of such artists as Louis F. Day, Walter Crane, C. F. A. Voysey and M. Mucha, this latter firm has done much to foster the beautiful in mural decoration, while in pottery they have been no less successful, the glazes of their Lancastrian ware being wonderful in their variety and quality.

It is not to be taken for granted that Staffordshire does not produce other than good pottery, good at least as far as the body and the potting are concerned, for there has been, and though in lesser quantities still is made, a cheap class of ware both in price and quality to supply certain demands. Large quantities of so-called art goods are produced as poorly conceived as they are executed, and the manufacturer finds consolation in the reflection that he is meeting a popular demand, and so long as the training necessary to distinguish pottery in good taste from the meretricious is absent this demand will continue to exist and be catered to. On the other hand, it is pleasant to be able to say that some of the smaller firms are making both china and earthenware every bit as good in quality as that made by the leading manufacturers.

With the potteries outside of Staffordshire we must deal very rapidly. The fine red clays of Devonshire are utilized in that county by a number of manufacturers, among whom are the Royal Tormohun Pottery, Torquay, established in 1880, who make a specialty of Devonshire folk lore, inscribing the quaint sayings on the pottery. Tormohun is the ecclesiastical name of the parish in which the pottery is situated. The Aller Vale Pottery, near Newton, also uses mottoes extensively, the decorations, like the Tormohun, being in colored slips. The Torquay Pottery Co. make goods on similar lines and also furnish a very beautiful and fine red body, largely used for decorating in oil colors. Charles H. Brannum, Barnstaple, which has long been the seat of a pottery industry, in his Royal Barum ware has struck a more original line. Slip painting and graffito are both employed, but the vari-colored glazes which are successfully employed tend to give this ware a certain originality. There are also potteries at Bovey, Tracey and other places.

Sir E. H. Elton, at Clevedon Court, produces much original work, characterized by artistic feeling, and his mat glazes are fine in texture and especially noteworthy.

The Burmantofts pottery, near Leeds (the Leeds Fire Clay Co.) make a large variety of ornamental pieces, always well modeled and finished in brilliant glazes.

Wm. Ault and Tooth & Co., at Burton, have both established for themselves reputations for good ornamental pottery which has sufficient individuality to command a good market. Tooth's yellow glaze has become a standard by which all other yellows are judged, and the mat glazes of Ault have perhaps no rival in England. The Church Gresley Potteries (T. G. Green & Co., Ltd.), were established in 1821 to manufacture cane ware from Derbyshire clay. Rockingham ware was added in 1860, and general earthenware in 1873, which necessitated the building of another factory. The pottery has been a success, and the present year has seen the installation of an electrical plant. The Cochrane pottery, of Glasgow, has been in existence over two hundred years. J. & M. P. Bell & Co., the Campbelfield Pottery Co., F. Grosvenor and John Thompson & Sons have also potteries here. The Nautilus Porcelain Co. turn their attention to ornamental articles in china. It is beautifully made, often no thicker than an egg shell.

Tamworth, in the south of Staffordshire, is the seat of a large terra cotta industry, Gibbs & Canning (established 1847), making a fine line of terra cotta, enameled in brilliant colors, called by them Della Robbia ware, for architectural use. George Skey & Co. make terra cotta of excellent workmanship and also stoneware. This by no means exhausts the list of potteries in England, for they are scattered throughout the three kingdoms, but producing nothing but ordinary staple goods, and which in the bulk of cases is not as good as the average Staffordshire ware they do not seem to call for individual mention.

CHAPTER XX.

FRANCE.

LIMOGES—HAVILAND & CO.—THE ALLUAUDS—PORCELAINES G. D. A.
—POUYAT—OLD ABBEY—OTHER FRENCH POTTERIES.

We have seen how the discovery of kaolin made Limoges the pottery center of France, though the decoration of the porcelain made there was done in Paris, the Limoges manufacturer simply making the ware, just as Staffordshire pottery was for a time sent to Liverpool to be printed. In neither case was it an economical arrangement and the adjustment was bound to come. In the case of Limoges the change was brought about by an American, David Haviland, another instance where an important

THE FIRST HAVILAND DECORATING SHOP. MOLD SHOP ON THE RIGHT.

pottery industry owes its success to foreign influence. It was in 1839, a quest he had been conducting to find the maker of a piece of unmarked china that had attracted his attention on account of the superiority of its paste, finally landed him at Limoges. This was a step accomplished, but the existing shapes were not suitable to the American market and he had to furnish models to the manufacturer who was with difficulty persuaded to consider such an innovation. Whilst his orders were being executed he organized a decorating shop—it was made out of a conservatory—employed skilled artists and pupils and in this manner started a business which has made the name Haviland & Co. famous the world over. Importations to America commenced in 1840, where the quality of the ware was quickly recognized, and from an average of

$100,000 in the first ten years, the exports in 1880 had reached a million and a half. This was the success that followed honest endeavor—a determination that the paste should be as good as the skill of the chemist could make it, the decoration suitable in character and artistically expressed and the craftsmanship beyond reproach. The manufacturing plant from a modest start grew rapidly, new factories have been built, modern labor-saving devices installed and upwards of twenty-five hundred people are

PORCELAIN.

now reaping the benefit of Mr. David Haviland's acumen and enterprise. Whilst the energies of the firm have been directed mainly to the production of utilitarian articles, in 1873, when Messrs. Chaplet, Laurin and Lafond originated the process of decorating the unbaked clay with colored slips, Mr. Haviland was quick to perceive its merits and with the resources at his command considerably improved it. Such artists as M. and Madame Bracquemond, Ringel, Noel, Aubé, Delaplanche, Lindener, Pallandre, and Ed and Al Dammouse by their artistic work rendered it a noteworthy production. It was an old method, it is true, but in Haviland's hands by its boldness of treatment and artistic freedom it became the forerunner of a number of imitators, establishing a school.

Then Mr. Haviland's attention was turned to *grès* in which larger pieces were possible, and an artistic success was attained and some very striking pieces made, some of which are illustrated here for the first time. The Persian blue of Nevers, which rivaled that of Persia, was also reproduced, and an impetus given to *grand feu* work in porcelain. There is no question as to the artistic success of these experiments, but they were a little in

GRÈS.   PORCELAIN.

advance of the times and the effort was abandoned, a decision the art lover has every reason to regret. It was the Havilands who introduced the chromo lithographic decorations on porcelain, a method since followed by practically every manufacturer in the world. Haviland porcelain is the standard by which all others are judged, and the success the house has achieved has been the result of honest endeavor accompanied by a determination not to pander to public taste but by artistic excellence to elevate it and encourage a love of the beautiful in articles of every-day use.

GRÈS.

Theodore Haviland was one of the partners in the firm of Haviland & Co., and when the dissolution of partnership took place, January 1, 1892, the old firm being reorganized as a stock company, Mr. Theodore decided to organize another company, and they erected a new factory, adopting all the most modern improvements and making it probably the most up-to-date pottery in Limoges. An efficient staff was organized, and in a very short time the new shapes and decorations were on the market and the success of the enterprise was never in doubt, the business steadily growing until it has assumed its present large proportions. It is distinctly a dinner ware house, and every energy is concentrated to maintain and improve their present standard of excellence. Once only did they depart from this rule, and that was for the Paris Exhibition, when some ornamental pieces were made which excited the most favorable comment.

We have before alluded to the Casseaux Works, founded by François Alluaud, the brother-in-law of the Girondist Vergniaud, in 1797, which passed into the hands of Charles Field Haviland in 1876, his wife being a granddaughter of M. Alluaud. Alluaud *père* was a man of considerable importance, being mayor of Limoges in 1792. In 1789 he was not only a representative in the General Assembly, but the director of the old Grellet factory, which had then come under the control of the Royal Manufactory of Sèvres (1789-1793). He had already found time to publish, in 1765, 1768 and 1769, several important technical books. He owned, and it is still in possession of the family, one of the most important clay mines in St. Yriex, founding a factory in 1797 or 1798. He died in 1799, and was succeeded by his son François, who continued his father's experiments, and brought them to a successful issue. The citizens of Limoges repeated the honor they had already conferred on his father, by electing him mayor of the city in 1830 and again in 1832.

THE ALLUAUDS.

Following the practice of the other Limoges manufacturers, the attention of the Alluauds was directed to the perfecting of the paste, but some experiments were made about 1815 in underglaze or "furnace fire" colors, very interesting examples of which are

EMPIRE SET, GRANDFEU, 1815.

to be seen in museums and private collections. Of about the same date is the Chinese shape, a very fine example of modeling, the details of which are unfortunately lost in the illustration. The body varies considerably from that of to-day, being almost pâte tendre.

Charles Field Haviland succeeded the Alluauds, and he was succeeded in 1881 by E. Gérard, Dufraissiex and Morel, afterwards changed to E. Gérard, Dufraissiex & Cie. January 4, 1901, this and the firm of Gérard, Dufraissiex & Abbot, of New

CHINESE SHAPE.

York, were consolidated and the entire business consolidated as a *société anonyme*, under the corporate title of Porcelaines G. D. A., the former partners being the sole stockholders, and the entire business placed in the hands of three directors, Emile Gérard, Jules Dufraissiex and Frank P. Abbot. Previous to this, early

A POTTERY PRIMER. 143

in 1898, an important change had been made in the trade mark, a change that only the most absolute confidence in both the artistic and intrinsic merits of their productions warranted, for they put aside all the aid and prestige that their established marks had given them, adopting an entirely different mark. There was much speculation at the time as to the wisdom of this, but time, the great arbitrator, has fully justified their courage.

M. Dufraissiex died in 1901, and the business was continued by the two remaining partners until 1907, when Mr. Abbot retired as a partner, shortly afterwards, however, resuming the management of the New York business.

The reputation M. Gérard had obtained in Limoges was fully sustained by the large business resulting and the technical advances made under his management, and in 1892 it was found necessary to entirely remodel and enlarge the works, its producing capacity being increased nearly 50 per cent. While primarily

DE FORESQUE WARE, 1895.

manufacturers of utilitarian ware Porcelaines G. D. A. has demonstrated its ability to produce artistic goods of an ornamental character, and their exhibits at the World's Fair and Paris included many exquisite examples of *feu de four*, which necessitates the employment of colors requiring the same heat as the body itself, thus securing the closest possible affinity, the great desideratum in all pottery. The colors were much brighter than any previously employed, and included pinks and delicate lilacs of beautiful tone and softness, the color so assimilated with the glaze as to render it impossible to separate them. Applied to table services the result is so distinctive as to warrant our regarding the process as a real advance in ceramics. In honor of the artist, George De Feure, this was called De Foresque ware and it included in addition to some good shapes in vases a number of exquisitely modeled animals, some of which

OLD ABBEY POTTERY.

The Old Abbey Pottery is housed in part of the monastery founded in the year 631 by St. Eloi, minister to King Dagobert, and which after being destroyed was rebuilt by the Emperor Charlemagne. Once celebrated for its beautiful enamels, it is now winning new honors in porcelain, part of the abbey having been turned into a pottery in 1810. The illustration shows the old abbey which is maintained by the Government, the pottery being housed in the quadrangle. The works were founded by Firmin Latrille, one of a group of men including Labesse, Raymond Laporte, Ardant and Perigault, who did much to establish the prestige of Limoges. Some of the old shapes, beautifully modeled and graceful in outline, are still in use. The recent developments have been quite rapid, and an aggressive policy combined with the application of artistic ideas, in conjunction with a fine body and glaze, are pushing the products of this pottery rapidly to the front.

The finely modeled jug illustrated, designed and modeled by Constant Sevin was produced about 1855 by Jouhanneaud and Dubois, now Jouhanneaud and Boudet, Limoges.

When kaolin was first discovered at St. Yriex, Pierre Pouyat had already a faïence factory there (about 1760). Recognizing the importance of the discovery, he bought a bed of the finest quality, and, purchasing the pottery, La Courtille, near Fontaine du Roi, Paris, he commenced manufacturing there, changing the character of the production altogether. It was one of the largest of the five Paris potteries and was founded in 1773 by Jean Baptiste Locre, who made hard porcelain in imitation of Meissen, and this led to the pottery being known as "Manufactur de Porcelain Allemand," and specimens of "Old Pouyat," including the well-known Barbeau pattern, are eagerly sought. The coulage or casting process was employed here as early as 1791, and at La Courtille they were the first to use *grand feu* colors. His son François, who had been associated with him, died in 1838, aged 86 years, and was succeeded by his son, J. Pouyat who, in 1842, built a factory at Limoges. At his death he was succeeded by his sons, Emile, Louis and Eugene. The Pouyat china is noted for its fine texture. Some cups of eggshell lightness attracted much attention and won for them the name of *tasses mousseline*, which has since become the accepted name for extremely thin cups.

In 1890 Emile Pouyat retired and was succeeded by Baron de la Bastide and M. Dubreuil. While still maintaining the quality of the paste, the trend of business necessitated the decoration of the ware, a not unfortunate circumstance, for Pouyat has given us some charming decorations, not only in services, but in the less utilitarian articles which serve to decorate our houses and by their beauty add to our aesthetic enjoyment.

The firm of Martin Frères was established in 1871 and was composed of Pierre and Charles Martin who withdrew from the Pouyat factory. At first they were decorators only, but later erected a pottery and manufactured their own china. On the death of Pierre Martin, the business passed entirely into the hands of Charles Martin, who is the present proprietor. The firm has shown considerable enterprise and some specimens of pâte-sur-pâte show much artistic feeling. They were among the first potters in France to produce incrusted gold patterns.

A. Lanternier, established 1885, succeeded his father, who had carried on a decorating business. M. Lanternier's early training was with the historic house of Wedgwoods, Etruria. His Trainon shape from its originality and beauty of line at once placed him high in the ranks of Limoges manufacturers.

M. Redon. Founded in 1853 by M. Martial Redon, and now conducted by his sons. M. Redon, for the valuable assistance he rendered to the Imperial China Works at St. Petersburg, was made Knight of St. Stanislas of Russia by Alexander III. M. Redon died in 1891. From 1867 to 1878 special attention was given to pâte-sur-pâte decorations, and the exhibit of this in 1878 showed some remarkable pieces in this style.

R. Delinières & Co., established about 1847 as a manufactory of white ware, a decorating department being added in 1881. M. Delinières, the founder, was one of the directors of the

Sèvres works. The firm was succeeded recently by L. Bernardaud & Co.

Chas. Ahrenfeldt started a decorating shop in 1884 and two years later commenced to make china. His son, Charles J., succeeded to the business. The body is one of the best made in Limoges, and a distinct effort has been made to depart from the stereotyped style of decoration and evolve something different. The illustration of their reproduction of the service made at Sèvres for Louis Philippe for the Château de Fountainbleau is a case in point and is beautifully executed.

There are many other factories in Limoges, among which may be mentioned La Seynie, Tressemanes & Vogt, L'union Céramique (Château china), the Elite works and W. Guerin & Co. Limoges china generally has earned for itself a high reputation, and while some of the makers receive here scant recognition it does not by any means follow that their productions are in any way less worthy of exploitation.

Scattered throughout France there are a large number of potteries producing earthenware and faience, the latter including some clever reproductions of the Rouen, Nevers and Strasburg schools. Those made by Jules and Courquin Fourmaintreaux, of Calais, occupy an honorable position. The potteries at Montereau, Creil, Longwy, Sarreguemines, Bordeaux and Choisy-le-Roi are under the control of the "Comptoir Céramique," an organization formed to regulate production and prices. Most of these potteries were founded by Englishmen, and while the first productions were good they soon degenerated, but were rescued from desuetude through the exertions of M. de St. Amand, assisted by Alexander Brongniart. The Bordeaux factory, founded in 1714, was closed by the Comptoir Céramique, but there is an independent factory there called "Fäiençerie Bordelaise," where decorated earthenware is made.

The initiative of the English style of earthenware in France is particularly due to Charles Leigh. His pottery at Douai was founded in 1781 and from here came one by one the overseers and workmen who created the potteries we have mentioned.

The soup tureen illustrated made at Longwy, from a design furnished by Napoleon I. is a good example of the period.

Clement Massier, Golf Juan, was one of the first to reproduce the *réflets métalliques* of the Persians, and is still unrivaled in them. His glazes in imitation of the secondary precious stones are wonderfully brilliant, and there is a decided individuality in his work, which is irresistible.

The old-established works at Luneville have been in the hands of Sebastien Keller and his descendants since 1786. Originally established in 1729 by Jaques Chambrette, it made such a good showing that in 1758 the king renewed the privilege previously granted and conferred on it the title "Manufacture Royale." Here were produced the best works of the sculptor Cyffle, who excelled in modeling rustic and popular types, the real and picturesque side of which he rendered in the happiest and most humorous mood.

These little faience figures, notwithstanding Cyffle's lack of education, show a thorough knowledge of modeling, an inherent skill and delicacy of touch which has given them a really artistic and intrinsic value. Had it not been for the wild and profligate life he led, Cyffle would undoubtedly have risen to greater heights. He died at Bruges in 1806 in obscurity and poverty.

The reproduction of Palissy pieces by Avisseau was the first of a series of efforts which initiated the ceramic renaissance in France, a movement that placed her as leader of the ceramic world. Some of the principal leaders in this are Theodore Deck, Emile Gallé, Lachenal, Delaherche, Damousse, Glatigny, etc.

Theodore Deck, in 1859, founded a small pottery in the Impasse des Favorites, Paris, where one b..

in a most masterly manner all the triumphs of former days and no ceramic puzzle seemed too difficult for him to solve. Persian faience of golden hue, the splendid carnation red of the Eastern potters, the glazes and enamels of the Chinese, the intricacies of the wonderful faience d' Oiron and reproductions of Hispano-Moresque ware followed each other with startling rapidity. The frontispiece of Palisay finished in colored glazes in which the beautiful blue known as Deck blue predominates in his creation and is said to be the largest piece of pottery ever made in Europe.

Perhaps no less important than that of Deck is the work of Emile Gallé of Nantes, who both in glass and pottery is producing work of the highest technical skill and artistic excellence. In this renaissance of the potter's art in France grès has been the favorite medium of these artist potters and with this simple material wonderful results have been obtained. The grotesque of Carriès, the works of Zeigler, Delaherche and Chaplet are all evidence of this. Pull and Barbizet, both of Paris, made fine reproductions of Palissy ware as well as more original creations. Sèvres uses grès largely and the bold and artistic pieces made are so much in advance of the ormula mounted and overloaded with decoration pieces formerly produced that one wonders how they were ever tolerated. M. Lachenal, too, uses this body and enriches it with flammé glazes, but this is only one of the mediums resorted to by this artist potter. *Pate-sur-pate*, glaze crystallizations and *réflets métalliques* spring like magic from his fingers. (See illustration, page 158.)

DECK POTTERY.

Taxile Doat has also done excellent work in both *grès* and *pate-sur-pate*. He is now connected with the Woman's Institution at St. Louis.

CHAPTER XXII.

HOLLAND—BELGIUM—NORWAY AND SWEDEN—ITALY—RUSSIA.
HOLLAND.

There were several manufactories of porcelain in Holland founded chiefly at that period when, owing to the Seven Years' War, the art languished in Germany. Of these the principal one was at Weesp, near Amsterdam, 1764 to 1781. It was reopened at Loosdrecht and then transferred to Amstel, but did not exist more than twelve or fifteen years. In 1778 a porcelain pottery was established at The Hague, but political events brought it to a close about 1793. The production was similar to that of Germany, but as it was restricted to home consumption it never assumed any importance.

The faience of both Amsterdam and Arnheim of the 18th century rivaled that of Delft. Of Delft we have already spoken. The "Porcelain Bottle" and "The Bell" were the only two potteries remaining in existence there in 1848, and in that year "The Bell" was silenced forever. The former, conducted by two sisters, led a precarious existence until about 1874, when Thooft and Labouchère bought it and with the assistance of M. Adolph Lecompte instilled new life in it, adapting the old Dutch methods to modern requirements. Whilst many reproductions have been made, much clever and original pottery, strong in character and perfect in technical skill, has been produced, and Delft has resumed its old position as a pottery producing center.

About 1885, a German nobleman, von Gudenburg, and Mr. Colenbrander, established the Rosenburg factory, which had no great success until 1893, when they were joined by J. J. Kok, who later became art director. He had a fine sense of form and color, but not much technical skill, and this induced him to collaborate with M. N. Engelen, an eminent chemist, and under this dual management the porcelain that astounded the world when first shown at the Paris Exhibition was produced. The body is an extremely fine one, the shape most original in form without being bizarre, and the decoration as original as the shapes. Masses of color are obtained, not by broad washes, but innumerable fine lines, part of the design being executed in *grand feu* colors and the remainder on the glaze. Casting is employed, the body being ex-

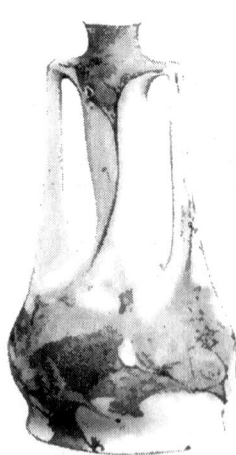

ROSENBURG.

tremely thin, and considering the acute angles in many of the pieces, their delicacy and the high heat at which they are fired, they must be regarded as evidence of the highest technical skill.

The De Distel Pottery produces a rich cream body, decorated with art noveau designs in liquid colors.

At Maastricht are the potteries of Petrus Regout and Co., one of the largest factories in the world producing earthenware on the English plan. They absorbed the house of Louis Regout and Co., porcelain manufacturers, but we have no information as to present production. There is also the Société Céramique at Wyk near Maastricht.

E. Estie & Co., Gouda, have produced, in earthenware, pieces similar in style and decoration to the Rosenburg ware, in addition to more original pieces with a combination of ornament and Dutch heads and landscapes in very soft and harmonious colors.

G. M. Augustijn, of the "De Kat" pottery, Bergen-ap-Zoom, produces an inlaid ware decorated in liquid colors very soft and harmonious in effect.

NORWAY AND SWEDEN.

Gustafsberg, an island in the Baltic Sea, about fourteen miles from Stockholm, has an interesting pottery. It was founded by Godenius about 1828, the commonest sort of ware being first produced. This was gradually improved and about 1850 wares similar to those made in England, including parian, were made. The island came into the possession of Mr. O. W. Odelberg, for twenty-three years a member of the Swedish Senate, and he conceived the idea of building a "Garden City" for his workpeople and to-day he is the ruler of over three thousand people, whose welfare, both morally, socially and physically is his particular care. Gustafsberg is in fact a kingdom in itself, a socialistic experiment which so far has yielded the happiest results. The man who is willing to work—and none other is tolerated—is free from the petty cares of life, no rent day stares him in the face, the education of his children is assured, and all reasonable opportunities afforded for his mental advancement. Even electricity to light his home is furnished him. Mr. O. W. Odelburg looks after the administrative part of the estate, the management of the pottery being vested in his son, Alex S. W. Odelburg. A comparatively young man, his energies have been bent to improving the quality of the wares and how the production can be simplified by machinery driven by electric power, the plant being eventually completely electrified.

The earthenware produced goes mostly to the Scandinavian market of which the firm has almost a monopoly for this class of ware. Recently a fine quality of bone china has been made which from its careful finish and artistic designs is destined to increase the prestige, it has already obtained. Associated with the pottery are a number of clever artists engaged in the decoration of vases and utilitarian articles, those illustrated being the work of Mr. Jekberg. (See illustration page 159.)

The Egersunda Faience Pottery, Christiana, makes earthenware similar to that of Sweden and china decorated in the classical manner prevalent in the north. There is also a porcelain factory at Porsgund.

The old Rörstrand pottery was founded in 1727. It was not at first very successful, but under the direction of Conrad Hunger, a Meissen decorator, assumed some importance. In 1735 the three crowns of Sweden were adopted as a trade-mark. The works were closed in 1788, but have been revived with very gratifying success. The productions vary from a fine quality of bone china to large ornamental pieces in majolica and services in earthenware. To make the product typical many distinctively Swedish designs have been carried out, the Swedish peasants portrayed and the works of Bellman, the Robert Burns of Sweden, utilized.

Much of the success of this pottery is due to Mr. Robert Alstrom, the director, the number of people engaged having risen from two hundred, when he took the reins of management, to over one thousand.

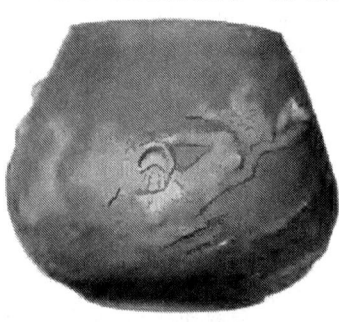

RORSTRAND VASE.

The pottery at Marieburg was founded in 1758, the products being of the Strasburg school. In striving for originality some curious and bizarre shapes were evolved, for instance a bishop's mitre was made to do duty as a soup tureen. The English printing process was adopted in 1765. The works were closed in 1780.

BELGIUM.

At the close of the eighteenth century there were two potteries at Ardenne, one of which produced some remarkable groups by Richardot, a celebrated Brussels modeler. Up to the beginning of last century a large business in printed earthenware was carried on there. Brussels in the eighteenth century made faience equal to either Normandy or Delft. Peterynck obtained in 1750 the privilege of manufacturing porcelain at Tournai, employing mostly English workmen. Some fine colors were realized and much imitation Sèvres ware was produced, the reproduction being very skilful. Boch Frères, La Louvière, are responsible for some remarkable work, their reproduction of Delft and Rhodian wares being especially noteworthy. They also produce tiles with crystalization of great depth and beauty. There is a pottery at Hasselt making colored glaze wares, and others at Viny and Quaregnon-Wasmuel.

RUSSIA.

Except in a few cases our knowledge of Russian ceramics is not in proportion to its extent, one Russian firm manufacturing china and earthenware, according to the London *Pottery Gazette*, which is generally well informed, finding employment for thirty thousand hands, which is far in excess of any other pottery in the world. In 1700 Peter the Great induced some Delft potters to start a works at St. Petersburg, and in 1700 another works was started at Revel by German workmen. This first factory or one contemporary with it was purchased by the Empress Elizabeth in 1756 and the manufacture of porcelain was commenced and has been uninterruptedly continued to the present day. Under Catherine II it was considerably enlarged, artists from Sèvres were engaged and the way was paved for the fine productions which have distinguished it. The paste is very hard and of a slightly bluish cast, but the prices demanded are so high that as far as bulk is concerned it has never assumed importance.

In 1835 Michael Kornilow established a china factory in St. Petersburg, the workmen being recruited from the Imperial works. From two kilns and about eighty workmen it has gradually increased in size and now covers thirty-five acres of ground and employs six hundred workmen. The kaolin used is from Glouchoff, province of Tschernigoff, the felspar from Finland and a clay from Borovitschi, Novgovod is also employed. The firm is now Kornilow Brothers. The body is a good one, equal to any made in Europe, and with its typical Russian style of decorations has created a good deal of favorable comment. It possesses a strong individuality, the handles and some of the shapes being characterized by striking originality. Figures in Russian costumes were made at Twer by Garnier about 1756. Korzec in Poland has had a porcelain works since 1803. An Englishman named Gardner established a pottery at St. Petersburg in 1789 and there are also works there owned by A. Popoff and M. Gulena. M. S. Kousnetrof & Co., Moscow, make Russian figures in native costume and Kusnettsoffs have a pottery about seventy miles from St. Petersburg, employing about 2,000 hands.

ITALY.

There are a great number of potteries in Italy, mostly producing goods of a mediocre character, and with few exceptions they do not call for special mention. In view of the prominent position once occupied by Italy in the ceramic world this is rather remarkable, as the potting instinct is not easily eradicated or its traditions forgotten. But had it not been for Ginori, Cantagelli and a few artist potters of whom Salvini is a type, its ceramic productions could have been briefly dismissed. Antibone de Nove and Raphael Passarin, of Bassano; the Castellanias, of Rome, and Laverno all deserve mention. The Signa pottery produces copies of antiques with an ivory finish; Mazzarelia, of Naples, pieces with fruits in high relief; Pesaro has several majolica factories, and the Florio family, the lords of Sicily, have a pottery producing hotel ware and a little china. Menghetti, of Bologna, works on similar lines to Ginori and his work is extremely good. Cacceapnote, of Naples, also does good work, earning the gold medal at the Milan Exhibition. The Cantagellis, of Naples, first came into notice in 1876, and followed up their initial success with very clever reproductions of Hispano-Moresque and early Italian wares, including the bas-reliefs of the Robbias. Mr. Ulysses Cantagelli, to whose enterprise the success the firm attained was largely due, died in 1901. The productions to-day run largely to architectural pottery.

RICHARD-GINORI.

To have built up an organization as powerful as that of the Richard-Ginori house, with its paid up capital of ten million francs and its four thousand employees, speaks volumes for the powers of organization of the present head of the firm, Commandatore Augusto Richard. His father, Giulio Richard, originally in a small way of business with his father was in 1841 admitted into the firm of Tinelli Brothers, who succeeded Gonrad, Father, Son & Co., established in 1830. It is interesting to note that Luigi Tinelli, one of the members of the Tinelli firm, in consequence of his taking an active part in the freedom of Italy movement was condemned to die, but the sentence was commuted by Francis I and he was exiled to America. He fought in the Civil War and was made a general for distinguished services. For a man of Richards temperament and ability the works at Milan, which only employed some five hundred workers, was far too small and in 1873 he effected the consolidation of potteries, which culminated in 1896, when the historic house of Ginori became a part of it. This consolidation marks an epoch in the history of Italian pottery, for thanks to Richard's ability and enterprise both the body and decorations were improved and modern methods superseded the old. Present day productions include those beautiful china services so distinguished in their perfection of modeling no less than for the classic designs which lend them distinction and which the immense size of the plant enable them to produce in generous quantities and which bear the impress of the centuries of experience which inspire them. There is scarcely a prince or potentate but whose table is graced with one of these services. From Doccia come immense quantities of insulators, another factory is devoted to tiles, another to earthenware and so on, each a specialist in their particular line and all under the management of the man who conceived the organization and brought it to a successful and profitable condition.

MARCHESE CARLO GINORI.

The foundation of the Doccia pottery near Florence by the Marquis Carlo Ginori, in 1735, was an epoch in the ceramic history of Italy. A hundred years had elapsed since the triumphs of Gubbio and Castel-Durante, which marked the culmination of the Renaissance. The discovery of hard porcelain by Böttcher, at Meissen, and its subsequent manufacture at other places, may have inspired Ginori to emulate their triumphs. From its inception it was marked by so much vigor as to make success certain. A ship was dispatched to China for the precious kaolin, and as early as 1737 Ginori was able to show specimens of his manufacture. The first productions showed the Oriental influence which at that time dominated all European porcelain, but very soon the love of creative art innate to the Italian asserted itself, and the Doccia Museum furnishes specimens of a more original character, including pierced vases and finely modeled groups, the date of which is about 1740. By the end of the century a very considerable advance had been made, the pieces, especially some lovely bas-reliefs, being more pretentious and showing that the potter had better control over his material.

Ginori seemed to take particular delight in showing how easily he could duplicate the triumphs of other potters. His reproductions of the best efforts of Sèvres and Meissen, including

REPRODUCTIONS OF SIXTEENTH CENTURY WARES.

the *pate tendre* of the former, if they did not possess the creative force of the originals, were at least evidences of technical skill. But perhaps his most noteworthy success in this direction was the reproductions of those Italian majolicas whose influence had been felt the world over. It was by no means an easy task, for artists had to be found who understood something of the spirit of such men as Maestro Giorgio, the Fontanos and others. Experiments with lusters and glazes had to be conducted, but eventually the perfection that Ginori demanded was obtained, and these replicas of sixteenth century art have a value all their own. The bas-reliefs of Lucca della Robbia were so well executed as in several cases to be taken for original works by that artist.

When the Capo di Monte pottery, founded in 1736, was moved to Buen Retiro, in 1759, there shortly afterwards came into the possession of Ginori a large number of molds of this celebrated pottery, and from them he has issued a number of reproductions in a special paste agreeing very nearly to that of Capo di Monte. We are thus, fortunately, able to obtain exact replicas of the productions of this interesting pottery.

On the death of the Marquis Carlo he was succeeded by the Marquis Lorenzo Ginori, in 1791, and direct descendants of this noble family for four generations have conducted the business, their lofty aspirations and steadfastness of purpose having caused the name of Ginori to take foremost rank among the potters of Europe.

Young readers will be interested to know that Monte Christo, the island made immortal by Dumas, belongs to the Ginori family.

CHAPTER XXIII.

DENMARK.

When the history of the Royal Porcelain Manufactory of Copenhagen comes to be written, it will be a record of perseverance, of absolute faith in its ultimate success, of long, weary years of struggling against adverse circumstances and opposition, such as is only paralleled by the story of the heroic Palissy.

Before its inception King Frederick V had a little factory, managed by Delhorn, a native of Saxony, and later by Fournier, a Frenchman. Only twenty pieces of the beautiful soft paste china made there are in existence.

Frantz Heinrich Müller, an apothecary and also master of the mint, had long had an ambition to make porcelain, but a chain of exasperating incidents prevented him making the attempt until September, 1773. The first firing was very disastrous, but three pieces had sufficient merit to warrant him presenting them to the King. He tried to raise a company, but succeeded only in selling one share, and the project must have been abandoned had not Privy Councillor Holm, secretary to the Dowager Queen Juliana Marie, came to his rescue. A few shares were sold, really a very trifling amount, and March 13, 1775, in spite of the opposition of the board of trade, he obtained a monopoly for Denmark. The working force was composed of soldiers and apprentices, and the following year this was augmented by three potters from Meissen, only one of whom showed any ability. Their arrogant conduct caused so much strife that Müller forcibly drove them from the factory, one of them being shortly afterwards readmitted. The capital at his disposal was so small that in order to secure the services of a modeler, Müller contributed a portion of his own salary, and A. C. Luplan, of Fürstenburg, was engaged. About this time, too, A. C. Bayer, who painted the Flora Danica service, was working there, though this service was not delivered until 1811. Later the force was augmented by Cleo, Sehman and the portrait painters, Cammeth and Omdrup. The financial part, in spite of the beautiful body compounded by Müller, was at a very low ebb, and April 21, 1779, the pottery was turned over to King Christian VII, who assumed its debts. Müller was made inspector, and the title of Councillor of Justice was bestowed on him.

Some exquisite groups and figures were produced, evidently the work of a repousse worker named Kallenberg, including some dancing figures, "The Flute Player," "Copenhagen Group" and others. These are generally credited to Luplan, but a letter of Müller's, recently come to light, proves otherwise. A term of prosperity ensued which lasted until the end of the eighteenth century.

Harassed by the English bombardment of the city in 1809 and by the economic misery that followed the pottery for a time led a pitiful existence. and in 1810 was actually closed down for a time for want of fuel. Müller was relieved of his onerous duties in 1801, but continued in an advisory capacity until 1811. He died in 1820, at a time when his beloved pottery for which he had given all he possessed in time, money and experience, was at the lowest ebb, only two painters being employed at the time, and the whole force consisting of about sixty people.

Prof. Mantley succeeded Müller, and in 1824 he was followed by Prof. G. Hetsch, who made a vigorous attempt to revive its falling fortunes. It was, however, impossible to adapt the body to the prevailing Empire style, and though large designs for monumental stands and vases are in existence, which were probably intended for the new Christiansberg Castle, they do not appear to have been carried out. The pottery was then intrusted to the postal authorities, but continued unremunerative. In 1848 the factory lost its Royal privileges and in 1887 was disposed of to A. Falcke for $15,000. He obtained permission to style it Royal. Holm was the administrator, and he succeeded in making it show a fair profit, though about the only thing of merit produced were the statuettes after Thorswalden. The fine body was obscured by decoration, the latter being much inferior to the former. In 1882 the pottery was resold to a limited company, "Aluminia," the owners of a large earthenware manufactory.

One of the earliest successes of the pottery was the fluted porcelain, decorated in blue, the Mussel pattern of the pottery, but known the world over as Danish pattern. Through many years it was the mainstay of the pottery.

158 SÈVRES.

FLORIAN, PAGE 134; LACHENAL, PAGE 148;
OTTO ECKMANN, PAGE 160; GUSTAVSBURG, PAGE 150;
JULIUS DIEZ, PAGE 167.

A POTTERY PRIMER.

When the Aluminia Company obtained the pottery, Mr. Phillip Schou, Councillor of State, was appointed director, and the pottery was removed in 1884 from the city to a site bordering the Frederiksburg Palace Gardens. He was fortunate enough to secure the services of Mr. Arnold Krog as artistic director and Mr. V. Englehardt, chemist. Both these gentlemen still honorably occupy their positions, but Mr. Schou retired in 1902, and

HIPPOPOTAMUS DESIGNED BY PRINCESS MARY OF DENMARK.

was replaced by Mr. Frederick Dalgas. Mr. Krog is an artist of undoubted talent and originality, Mr. Englehardt a thorough chemist, and between them they astonished the world when their display at Copenhagen was seen in 1888. It was something new in European ceramics, and the wonderful part was that so much had been accomplished by such simple means. Every piece was in itself an *objet d'art*, so direct and so simple that it forced recognition. The beautiful body of the ware had been preserved instead of hidden, and enhance the charm of the few simple colors employed by skilled artists in its decoration. The firing had been carried so high that the colors completely amalgamated with the glaze, and a softness of effect was produced never before approached. This exhibit placed Copenhagen at one step at the head of the ceramic industry, and its influence on modern ceramics has been such as to

DANISH PLACQUE.

have no paralfel in history. Many of the vases and placques signed by the artist are never reproduced. A great success was attained by the beautifully modeled figures and animals, which have been extensively imitated, but the dominant note in them —the aliveness, to coin a word, has been conspicuous by its absence. The first piece made was a codfish.

When Mr. Schou and Mr. Krog came into office it was with a determination to produce something different from existing pottery, but something that should at the same time be artistically ceramic. Together they journeyed through Europe, but without result, until they happily saw the Oriental collection of Herr S. Bing, which showed them that the possibilities of decorative art had been realized. Lusburg, the sculptor, was appointed modeler, and Hallem his assistant and the work commenced. Of Mr. Schou it may be said that had it not been for his initiative, industry and resourcefulness the factory would hardly have been in existence at the present day. He alone possessed all the qualities necessary to raise this monument to Danish art and culture.

The Copenhagen crystalline glazes were discovered by Clemart, the chemist, and perfected by his successor, Herr Englehardt, and these led the way to those of Sèvres and Berlin.

The earthenware made at the Aluminia factory, initiated by Mr. F. Dalgas, is also remarkable. The difference between a porcelain and an earthenware body is rightly recognized in the style of the decoration. It is more robust in treatment, brighter in color and more inclined to the conventional.

There was a faïence manufactory at Kiel, founded about 1760 by John Buchwald, and good work was produced, notably that of a painter named Leihamer.

Madame Ipsen, of Copenhagen, produces copies of Greek vases and statuettes in terra cotta, both very finely and artistically executed.

Wendrich & Sons, also of Copenhagen, produce goods of a similar character.

There is a tile factory producing both floor and wall tiles at Hakkema.

The house of Bing & Grondahl, Copenhagen, founded in 1853, has attained distinction under the administration of Mr. Willumsen, appointed in 1897. Some of the artists who assisted in this are Hollin, Patersen and H. Kofoed. A beautiful pink is a characteristic of their crystalline vases and *grand feu* porcelain. They also produce a large number of beautifully modeled animal figures, very soft in coloring.

CHAPTER XXIV.
GERMANY AND AUSTRIA.

Next to England, Germany is the largest pottery-producing country in the world. The products cover the whole field of ceramic art. We have seen that it is to Germany we owe the introduction of the manufacture of porcelain in Europe; and while many of the old factories no longer exist, the number of new ones is legion. About 45 per cent. of the German potteries are in Prussia, 10 per cent. each in Saxony, Bavaria and Anhalt, and 8 per cent. in Saxe-Weimar. The exports for 1909 were $18,750,000. The industry must be on a firm basis, the shares of six of the leading porcelain factories being quoted at an average of 90 per cent. above par, some of them paying as high as 18 per cent. dividend.

We can only very briefly notice a few of the best-known houses, giving more especial attention to those producing goods of an ornamental character. Nor is it to be surmised that this includes all worthy of notice, and we have two special productions in mind, for it often happens that information is withheld by those able to give it for purely commercial reasons.

The old Fürstenburg pottery has been revived and is producing good work.

The Ph. Rosenthal Co., Selb., produces porcelain of excellent quality, the shapes being original in thought, well modeled and carefully potted.

The Tirschenreuth Porcelain Factory was founded in 1835 and employs about 500 hands.

Majolica of good quality is made at Carlsruhe, at the Grand Ducal Majolica Factory, which maintains an efficient artistic staff, among whom may be mentioned Thomas, Suss, Janssen and Binser.

Count von Thuns has an old established porcelain works at Klosterle on the Elbe, Karl Merker, the director, having this year completed 50 years of efficient service.

Ressner & Kehhel, Turn, are the manufacturers of the popular and well-known Amphora ware.

Springer & Co., Elbogen, were established in 1815. They make a large variety of useful and ornamental goods and employ over 1,000 workpeople, and theirs is probably the largest factory in Austria.

Moritz Fischer in 1830 established a manufactory of porcelain at Herend (Hungary) whose original productions equaled anything made in Europe. So clever were his reproductions of Oriental porcelain that they were often mistaken for originals, a cabaret of his being purchased by the South Kensington Museum as a valuable Oriental piece. The present proprietor is Eugene de Fischer, and the reputation of the firm is worthily upheld by him.

W. Zsolnay, Funfkirchen, established in 1835, uses the five churches as his trade mark. Mr. Zsolnay is a potter of great ability, and his *reflets des metalliques* are superb in their brilliancy. Every year he demonstrates his progressiveness, and his mark is accepted as an indication that the piece of which it is impressed has a value beyond its mere commercial one.

The old works at Lembach (Saxe Meningen), founded about 1770, are still in existence, as are also those at Nymphenburg.

F. A. Mehlem, Bonn, established 1755, is a large and progressive pottery employing 700 to 800 workmen. He makes both china and earthenware and some very fine pieces are produced, though the bulk of the product is "commercial art."

REPRODUCTIONS OF DRESDEN FIGURES—SCHIERHOLZ.

At Carlsbad there is a large quantity of porcelain produced, the manufacturers principally catering to the cheaper markets. At Pirkenhammer is the pottery of Fischer & Meig, who are in a different class, and whose work has a well-deserved reputation.

Rudolstadt is the home of the New York and Rudolstadt Pottery Co., almost entirely devoted to works of art. A large and efficient staff of artists is employed, who find an exercise for their talents in the decoration of vases, many of the figure-subjects being beautifully executed. Here also are the works of Beyer & Boch and E. Blome & Son, who make tinted figures. Schafer & Vater are also located there.

J. von Schwarz, of Nuremburg, is a manufacturer whose fine colored glazes are marvels of the potter's art, his color schemes being both beautiful and original. Dr. Richard Lindhurst is the director.

The manufacture of porcelain stoves is an important factor

in German ceramics. Among others, the Seltzmans, of Oberdorf, produce them.

Ludwig Wessell, Popplesdorf, has produced much finely decorated ornamental porcelain, enriched with gold relief work, very carefully executed and with commendable restraint.

Wolfsohn, Dresden, for some time marked his wares with the Meissen Caducus and the monogram A. R. until stopped by litigation. The mark is now a D under a crown.

The Emperor of Germany is the proprietor of the Cardinen pottery, but no pieces made there have come under our observation.

Scattered all over the country are large numbers of stoneware potteries.

DRESDEN REPRODUCTIONS—STYLE OF 1760.

C. G. Schierholz & Son, Plaue, Thuringia, make a large assortment of goods, mostly in the style of Dresden, the work all being done by hand, no printing or transfers being used. They have also successfully reproduced a number of Dresden groups and statuettes, adapting some of these for electric light portables.

The vases illustrated are reproductions of the style of 1760, which is distinguished by the use of a black outline.

VILLEROY & BOCH.

The reputation attained by Germany in the manufacture of stoneware is worthily maintained, and we may without hesitation say been enhanced, by the house of Villeroy & Boch, an amalgamation of interests for the beginning of which we must go back to 1748, when Pierre Joseph Boch established a pottery in Hayingen (Lorraine), which he was obliged to abandon on account of an unsuccessful law suit. In 1766 a him and his brother by the Austrian government, and a pottery was built at Septfontaines, the concession carrying with it the right to use the Austrian arms as a trade mark, though the blue and white earthenware made at this period is usually marked with the intertwined letters B. L. (Boch, Luxemberg). Pâte tendre was made in 1790, but in ornaments and small figures only. This pottery was destroyed in 1795 during the siege of Luxemberg. It was rebuilt immediately after peace was declared. Boch died in 1818. In 1789 Nicolas Villeroy, a native of Metz, gave up a pottery at Frauenberg (Alsace) to start one at Wallerfangen, the first important progress being the adoption of the English process of manufacture, under the French engineer Aug. Jaunez, appointed in 1828. Up to this time the production was similar in character to the wares of Rouen, etc., the body being covered with a tin enamel, which we term faïence.

Jean Francis Boch, who succeeded his father, through purchase came into possession of the old abbey at Mettlach (Rhenish Prussia), which had been suppressed soon after the French revolution. It dates from the second half of the sixth century, though some of the existing buildings which are standing to-day were erected much later, some as late as 1737-1771. The turning of the abbey into a pottery contained the important provision that only hard coal should be used, no doubt to promote the workings of the extensive coal lands in the immediate vicinity. Wood had hitherto been the only fuel used for firing pottery, and it must have necessitated some courage in his own resources to accept such a condition. It was no easy task, and Boch had almost as many trials and disappointments as that synonym for perseverance, Bernard Palissy, but happily he succeeded and attained the distinction of being the first potter to introduce coal as a fuel for firing pottery on the continent of Europe. It was soon afterwards adopted by Villeroy, of Wallerfangen. While solving this problem, Boch had also the management of the pottery at Septfontaines on his shoulders and found time, too, to perfect a waterpower system for turning the potters' wheels, doing away with the laborious and distracting use of his foot by the potter. It was at Mettlach, too, that the English system of printing in underglaze colors was first introduced on the continent of Europe. The early Mettlach production was a soft calciferous body, but about 1832 the lime was replaced by felspar, making a much more durable body, and later this was in turn improved.

In 1841 the three factories, Wallerfangen, Septfontaines and Mettlach, were consolidated, and soon afterwards the manufacture of decorative stoneware was commenced at Mettlach, a manufacture for which they have since been regarded as its best exponent. At first the ornamentation was solely in relief, partly done on the mold and partly by separate modeling. A later example of this latter is the jug with vine decoration made for Emperor William I.

But the reputation of the firm after all rests mainly on the "Chromolith" ware, introduced about 1863, for it enabled them to produce ware of the highest artistic excellence by an entirely new method and giving entirely new effects, a method which is distinctively their own and which has never been successfully imitated or its method of production discovered. The ornamentation is inlaid in colored clays, much in the style of cloisonne enamel. The best artists in Germany have furnished designs which skilled craftsmen at the pottery have faithfully reproduced. While the original idea was in itself wonderful enough, the cost was quite

ARTISTIC STONEWARE JUG.
Made for Emperor William I.

VASE IN PARIAN.
Made in 1854 for the Crown Prince.

high, and therefore the subsequent simplification of the method which made it a commercial article within the reach of all may justly be classed as the more important of what we may regard as two distinct inventions.

In addition to this stoneware, earthenware services in a large variety of designs and fancy goods were also made, and in 1850 architectural terra cotta was introduced. Parian was made in 1851, following closely its introduction in England. The piece illustrated was made in 1854 for the Crown Prince of Prussia, later Emperor William of Germany. The Wadgassens factory, which makes glassware only, was founded in 1841, and the Mettlach Mosaic Tile Work in 1869. A new pottery was built at Dresden, where dinnerware, wall and hearth colored glazes and sanitary goods are made. At Merzig, founded 1879, are made the terra cotta architectural ornaments and life-size figure subjects, mostly of religious subjects. At Schramberg, founded 1833, white earthenware and ornamental objects in majolica are produced, and finally, in 1907, the pottery at Daneschburg was acquired. These potteries have all been successful and are a lasting tribute to the resourcefulness of the men who have conducted them and who have very largely stood in a parental at-

AMPHORA IN TERRA COTTA.
Made for Empress Augusta.

CHROMOLITH VASE.
One of the First Mettlach Inlaid Stone Productions.

titude towards the 10,000 workpeople employed. Jean François Boch died in 1858, but since 1852 his oldest son, Eugene, has been in charge. For his services to German ceramic art, in 1892, Emperor William II bestowed on him the inheritable state of nobility, receiving the title of Privy Councillor. His son, René, was director-general of the combined potteries until his death in 1908, when his son, Dr. Roger von Boch, succeeded him, Lentwere von Boch acting in his place when he is absent. Edmund, brother of René, was director of the Mettlach works from 1867 to 1908.

The care of the workpeople seems to be as important in the eyes of the management as its commercial or artistic success, and for their use hospitals have been endowed, schools and nurseries maintained, gymnasiums and swimming baths provided. The widows and orphans are provided for, and there is a pension fund for those whose years of service entitle them to reward. There are sleeping rooms and a restaurant, where for 14 cents a day board and lodging can be obtained. The firm will also build houses for their employees on the easiest possible terms. The result of this interest in their employees is that such a thing as a strike is unknown, that the majority grow old in their service, there is respect and affection on both sides and everyone gives his best to enhance the success of the whole.

There has been a notable advance in German ceramics during the last few years. A better understanding of the laws of decoration is apparent and the coloring is more subdued and harmonious. Professor Lauger introduced a pre-Raphaelite style, its simplicity and directness immediately commanding attention. One of the best uses to which this was put was its application to stoves.

Julius Diez, of Villengen, in the Black Forest, has only recently devoted himself to ceramics, but the distinctly decorative character of his production, in which fantasy and humor are combined, make them objects of delight. It has truly been said of him that "Diez is a German primitive in his art, and his essentially German interpretation of the world around him is manifest from these most recent products of his talents, for we see in these ceramic designs at once the individual and the nation to which he belongs." (See illustration page 158.)

Hermann Mutz and his son Richard, at Altoona, a suburb of Hamburg, are producing glazes of the greatest brilliancy, surpassing anything of the kind heretofore made in Germany. Mostly for utilitarian purposes, they show great ingenuity of form. (See illustration page 158.)

At one time associated with Professor Lauger was a chemist of Munich, Max von Heider, but the latter, incurring the displeasure of Professor Lauger, was banished from his workshop. Von Heider then associated himself with his three sons, Hans. Fritz and Rudolph, three well-known sculptors and painters. They produced some remarkable pottery, though the shapes are somewhat forced and altogether lack the simplicity that characterizes Lauger's work. Art Noveau decorations are freely used, but here again the pieces lose their value by the eccentricity

CHAPTER XXV.
UNITED STATES.

Various scattered and isolated attempts were made in America to establish the potters' art, but were for the most part ephemeral and had no influence on the art of to-day. A Staffordshire potter named Bartlem made an unsuccessful attempt in South Carolina about 1765, and in 1771 it was reported in England that in Philadelphia "better cups and saucers are made than at Bow or Stratford." Several attempts were made in Connecticut, Charles Lathrop, Norwich, 1796; Isaac Hanford, Hartford, and Adam States, Stonington, and also at Morgantown, W. Va.

About the middle of the eighteenth century John Crolius, who was succeeded by his son, Clarkson, and John Remmey, were both making salt-glaze stoneware at Potters' Hill, where the New York Hall of Records now stands. Potters' Hill was leveled about 1812, when the Collect Pond was filled up. Remmey's descendants were making salt-glaze stoneware in Baltimore in 1823-4, and afterwards moved to Philadelphia, where the business is now carried on. Perrine & Co. were also making stoneware in Baltimore about the same time.

In 1800 the clay at South Amboy was being used by Van Weckle, and a little later by Price, of Sayerville.

In 1825 a number of Frenchmen commenced the manufacture of artificial china at Jersey City, but it was not a success, and production ceased after a year or two. In 1829 the works were reopened by David & J. Henderson, and in 1833 a company known as the American Pottery Co. was formed.

The printing process was used here for the first time in America. Daniel Greatbach, a good modeler, worked here and produced a jug with hunting subjects in relief, with a hound handle. The same motif had been used years before in England, but it proved very popular and has been reproduced or imitated several times. Another change took place in 1845, and the firm became Rhodes, Strong & McGerron. In 1855 they sold out to Rouse, Turner, Duncan & Henry, and a little later Rouse & Turner carried it on alone. The works were demolished in 1892. Earthenware and Parian were made, and some of the Parian jugs are exceedingly good. (Illustration page 158.)

THE "HOUND" JUG.

Some time between 1816 and 1827, W. T. Tucker was making porcelain in Philadelphia, being awarded a medal by the Franklin Institute in the latter year. Judge Hemphill acquired an interest in the business, and on the death of W. E. Tucker continued it in conjunction with Thomas Tucker, afterwards selling out to the latter. The works were closed in 1838. The product was principally table services, the body and glaze of fair quality, but the decorations were in no way remarkable. Foreign competition proved too much for the infant industry, and it consequently died of public neglect.

In 1830, Smith Fife & Co. exhibited some porcelain at the Franklin Institute, Philadelphia, but nothing is known of them and it is possible they were decorators only. One of the specimens marked as manufactured by them is a plate. This presupposes a considerable mechanical equipment, but there is no such firm mentioned in the Philadelphia directories of that year.

BENNETT ALBION WARE.

Kurlbaum & Schwartz, Philadelphia, made china of good quality from 1851 to 1855. The works were on Front street.

In 1834 James Bennett built a small pottery at East Liverpool, O., making common wares, in no way remarkable, but which had a decided interest, for it marked the foundation of a pottery center which has assumed such proportions that it is to-day the principal seat of the industry in America. In 1837 Bennett was associated with James Clews in the disastrous enterprise at Troy, Ind. He died in 1862. His brother, Edwin, built a pottery at Baltimore about 1844, which has since assumed importance. Parian was made from 1884 to 1887, in addition to majolica, Rockingham, etc. In 1890 the business was incorporated, and under the management of Mr. Henry Brunt, a decidedly progressive step was made. Apart from the regular commercial production of dinner and toilet ware, their most notable successes were a beautiful combination of colors in a glaze called Brubensul and the slip-patented Albion ware. (See page 169.) Theirs was the first house in America to successfully compete with foreign makers in the production of steins. At Baltimore, also, is the pottery of D. F. Haynes & Son, started in 1881. It is known as the Chesapeake Pottery, and Edwin Bennett was at one time interested in it. The productions, principally utilitarian ware, were marked by originality. A very large business was done in clock cases, and for some years these had a tremendous vogue. Ground laying with an air brush was used here for the first time in America.

In Bucks and Montgomery counties, Pennsylvania, a slip-decorated ware was made by Germans from the last half of the eighteenth to the middle of the nineteenth century. While very rude in design and execution, it is interesting as showing the expression of an art feeling among an uncultured people.

Some time prior to 1825, a pottery was started at Mill Creek, between Southall and Greenport, L. I., by Austin Hempstead. The products were principally pie dishes and other articles of utility in brown earthenware decorated with white slip, often the name of the owner. The large conical molds for making loaf sugar were also made here. The pottery is only interesting as an illustration of the resourcefulness of the early settler, and it was built to help furnish a cargo for the brig "Stirling," built to ply between Greenport and the West Indies, for the colonists had little to offer in the way of exchange for molasses, rum, etc., except barrel staves. The pottery was closed in 1868. Austin Hempstead founded the town of Hempstead in Nassau County.

In 1846, white, yellow and Rockingham ware were made at Bennington, Vt. In the second phase of the pottery, Lyman & Fenton were the proprietors, and in 1849 it became the United States Pottery. Parian groups and figures were made, some of them rather quaint; others without much merit, either as to modeling or conception, and the pottery only existed until 1858. Daniel Greatbach worked there and reproduced his hound-handle pitcher, varying the top somewhat.

A POTTERY PRIMER.

In 1848 Charles Cartlidge was making china door furniture and buttons by the Prosser process at Greenpoint, L. I., and a little later table ware, at first in bone china and later in hard porcelain. Frank Lockett and Elijah Tatler were employed as painters, the latter afterwards founding the Tattler Decorating Co., of Trenton, N. J. Josiah Jones, the modeler, was a capable man, and his works are produced both in Parian and Jasper ware. He executed a number of busts and bas relief of American prominent men. In 1855 the firm was dissolved and reorganized as the American Porcelain Manufacturing Co., with Mr. Cartlidge as president, but no success was attained and the works were closed in 1856. There was probably more promise here than had up to that time developed in any other American pottery venture, but the productions were probably in advance of the times.

BENNINGTON POTTERY.

In 1854 the Union Porcelain Works was started at Greenpoint by a number of German workmen, but owes its success to Thos. C. Smith, who joined them in 1867. Bone china was made until 1863, which was replaced by a purely Kaolinic body in 1865. Karl Muller modeled some ambitious pieces, among which may be mentioned the "Century" and "Keramos" vases. A very good china body is produced, and the firm has the distinction of being the only one in America to make a true porcelain.

The year 1852 marks the initiation of pottery making in Trenton, N. J. Taylor & Speeler, who made Rockingham and yellow ware, being the pioneers. In 1855 they produced the first white granite made in America. Astbury & Millington in 1853 were the first to make sanitary ware. The same year the firm of W. Young & Sons, afterward Willett was founded, and others followed in the order named: 1859, Rhodes & Yates; 1863, Etruria Pottery; 1863, Coxon & Co., John Moses and the Greenwood Pottery Co.; 1869, Mercer Pottery; 1879, Willetts; 1879, Burroughs & Montford and the International Pottery; 1893, Maddock Pottery Co. and the Ceramic Art Co., now Lenox, Ltd., in 1889.

The Greenwood Pottery Co., after many weary months of disappointment, succeeded in making a vitrified earthenware for hotel use and which may be claimed as a distinctly American invention. It combines the best qualities of both porcelain and earthenware with a minimum of their objectionable qualities. In spite of the apathy of the trade, James Tams, who was the leading spirit of the firm, succeeded in introducing it, and its merits once known a constantly increasing demand has existed, so that two other potteries had to be added to keep pace with it. Some experiments were made with art goods, but the body was not suitable and the effort was abandoned.

The Etruria Pottery (Ott & Brewer) in 1875 secured the services of Isaac Broome, whose busts and figures in Parian are highly esteemed. A little later, William Bromley, who had been identified with the manufacture of Belleek, both at Stoke and in Ireland, was engaged, and the manufacture of Belleek was commenced and carried to a satisfactory conclusion, the product equaling the original. The process is very simple, the ware receiving simply a wash of luster and fired in the enamel kiln at a low heat. These lusters were invented by J. H. Brainchou, and were sold by him to the Belleek Pottery and anyone else who wished to use them. To-day they can be bought from any dealer in ceramic supplies. Ott & Brewer unfortunately were not able to weather the financial crisis of 1892-3, and the works were closed.

Burroughs & Montford produced some fine pieces reminiscent of Doulton, as did the Maddock Pottery Co. In the case of Burroughs & Montford the ware was not equal to the decoration, and the losses that ensued caused the dissolution of the firm.

After the passing of the Wilson tariff bill a very general improvement was noticeable in the Trenton productions generally. The body and glaze were brought into closer affinity, to the benefit alike of manufacturer and purchaser.

The Ceramic Art Co., Trenton, N. J., was established in 1889. Walter S. Lenox has always been the dominant factor in the firm, and in 1896 the business virtually passed into his hands. Belleek ware was successfully produced, a fine bone china body being used. Many skilled artists were employed in the painting of vases with figures and other subjects in the then prevailing style, but the company, which is now known as Lenox, Inc., has practically abandoned this branch of the business and now devotes its energy to services for the table.

James Ca., had a pottery in South Amboy from 1852 to 1854, when it was burned down. Druggists' jars and boxes were the principal production. In 1855 he opened a pottery in West Thirteenth street, New York, making Rockingham and yellow ware until 1858, when white granite was added. Some experiments were made in bone china, but it proved too expensive to manufacture advantageously. Majolica and Parian were also produced—not of a very high order of merit if judged from the standards of to-day, but creditable efforts for the time.

The New England Pottery Co., of Boston, was founded in 1854, but did not achieve any distinction until 1886, when L. W. & Thomas Gray secured the services of Thomas Copeland, a modeler and decorator who produced some excellent shapes in small pieces. The designs proved popular, especially when treated in a deep, rich blue finished in gold. When Mr. Copeland left the company in 1895 the manufacture of these artistic pieces was abandoned and cream color ware is now the staple product.

At Wheeling, W. Va., the Wheeling Potteries Co. was incorporated in 1879, and under the management of C. W. Franzheim had for many years a prosperous existence, their services in cobalt blue and gold being very attractive. It was the first firm who had the courage to exploit their wares as "made in America," but it proved somewhat of a boomerang, as manufacturing difficulties were encountered which so damaged their reputation that the works were closed in 1908. Allied to them was the Vance Faience Co., who after costly experiments in a number of directions, eventually made a really attractive line of slip-decorated ware in conventional designs, but owing to the poor potting it had to be abandoned. The pottery is now engaged in the manufacture of bathtubs.

The Warwick China Co., of Wheeling, was organized in 1887, and it made a notable success under the management of Thomas Carr, son of the James Carr before mentioned, from 1893 to 1909, when he retired. The body is one of the best made in America, and a great commercial success has been made with their line of novelties, viz., those pieces which while possessing utilitarian qualities are not included in the composition of dinner services. Charles E. Jackson succeeds Mr. Carr in the management.

Following the effort of James Bennett, the Harker Pottery Co. was founded in East Liverpool in 1840; the Goodwin Pottery Co. in 1844; Knowles, Taylor & Knowles, 1853; Vodrey, 1857; C. C. Thompson, 1868, and all are now in existence. Up to 1872 Rockingham and yellow ware were the only wares made, but in that year Knowles, Taylor & Knowles commenced to make white ware. This firm in a few years grew from a one-kiln plant to such proportions as to necessitate the employment of upwards of 1,000 hands. When Joshua Poole became the practical potter he introduced a fine china body called Lotus ware, but, excellent as it was, it was not found possible to market it advantageously and it was consequently abandoned.

The firm of Laughlin Bros. was established in 1874 at East Liverpool, and for several years a thin translucent china was produced, but was abandoned in 1889, and an earthenware body of fine quality was substituted. The firm, from their good shapes and careful workmanship soon assumed importance. The firm was incorporated in 1897 as the Homer Laughlin China Co., building an additional plant at Newell, W. Va., and have the largest plant in the United States.

There are many other potteries in addition to those already enumerated, but on account of the similarity of the goods produced they do not call for special mention. The difficulties our potters experienced in the early years are gradually disappearing, the body and glaze now being excellent, but there is room for a greater initiative in the decoration. About the only firms who employ the process of printing from copper plates, on which the foundation of the prestige of English earthenware principally rests, are Mayer Bros., of Beaver Falls, and the Buffalo Pottery Co., the remainder of the American manufacturers relying for their designs on chromo lithographs, and it is not unusual for the same pattern to be sold to more than one manufacturer.

In a class by themselves are the Onondaga and Iroquois potteries of Syracuse, the former founded in 1871. Under the able management of James Carr, the Onondaga is firmly established, its hotel china being known from Maine to California. In 1891 some ornamental pieces were made, which were designated as "Imperial Geddo," but its manufacture had to be abandoned on account of the increased demand for its table ware.

The Wannopee Pottery, New Milford, Conn., founded in 1890 (having been known from 1887 as the New Milford Pottery Co.) commenced making colored glaze pottery and green lettuce ware, but had only a short existence, which is to be regretted as their shapes were good and their glazes most attractive.

The Buffalo Pottery Co. make a specialty of underglaze decoration and some finely engraved designs of Old English subjects under the name of Deldare have proved very successful. Practically in all its details of workmanship and the use of materials this pottery is conducted on English models.

The Pope-Gosser China Co. made a radical and successful departure in their shapes, adopting those of the silversmith with such modifications as the material demanded.

ROOKWOOD.

In all countries of the world the potters' art has been fostered and encouraged by ruling potentates. From the very beginning the Chinese emperors poured forth their treasures to assist it. The Prince of Satsuma rendered possible the celebrated Corean pottery. The Medicis and other noble Italian families were intimately identified with the renaissance of the potters' art in Italy; Augustus II. financed the experiments of Böttcher, who gave Europe its first porcelain; the French emperors made possible the glories of Sèvres, and George I. depleted Saxony to assist Chelsea. In America the patronage of those best able to bestow it is conspicuous by its absence, and "Made in America" seemed a reproach rather than a recommendation. The production of pottery was as a result of mediocre character. There was a tremendous breach into which no one dared to step. Such conditions have existed before, and it is interesting to note from what sources help has come. From the potter himself? Palissy was a glass painter; Helene de Hengest, a lady of quality and her principal assistant, a librarian; Lucca della Robbia was a sculptor; Böttcher, an apothecary; Dr. Wall, a chemist; Haviland, an importer; Deck and his confrères, all artists, and William de Morgan, a painter. It was a woman who in America dared to leap into the breach and give us an art. Mrs. Bellamy Storer commenced her experiments in 1876, and finally in a pottery of her own in 1880, on Eastern avenue, Cincinnati. The dominant idea was to produce something that should owe nothing to foreign influence; should be made of native materials and without mechanical aid. The artists were recruited from the School of Design; the shapes, except in very exceptional instances, thrown and turned. After countless disappointments the ware now known as "Standard Rookwood" was evolved. Taking the piece to be decorated in its clay state, just hard enough to handle without injury, the artist painted on it in various colored clays whatever his or her artistic instinct suggested. This was then fired, covered with a rich glaze and fired again. The idea was by no means new, for the Romans used the same process, and the old English potter revived it. But the Rookwood ware demonstrated how little those who formerly

TILE PANEL.

used the process knew of its possibilities. It was a revelation; something entirely new, for its prototype need not be considered. The harmony of color, the restraint in decoration and the luscious softness of the glaze gave to the painting the appearance presented by a pebble under limpid water. So charmed was the eye that another sense was involuntarily called into play: you feel compelled to touch it. Gladstone must have had some such feeling when he expressed the beautiful simile, "soft as the touch of a baby's hand."

In 1883 Mrs. Storer was fortunate enough to associate herself with W. W. Taylor, whose knowledge and courage supported her in many moments of disappointment, and who has continued to be the guiding spirit of Rookwood to the present time.

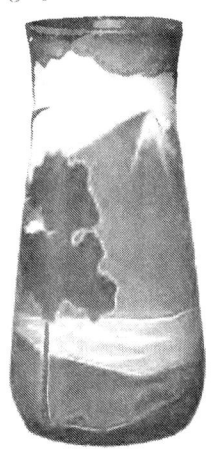

ROOKWOOD VELLUM.

Joseph Bailey, who evolved many of the colors used, also rendered invaluable aid, and his death in 1898 was a severe loss. It was in this year that for the first time the pottery became self supporting, and after nine years of strenuous fighting, having accomplished the work she had set out to do, having demonstrated the possibilities of American art pottery, Mrs. Storer withdrew her aid and the business was transferred to a company under the control of Mr. Taylor. In 1892 a new factory was built on the bluff of Mount Adams, overlooking all lower Cincinnati.

While a great success had been attained—a success in which critics all over the world joined—Rookwood was not content to rest on its laurels. The native clay had inclined its color to reds and browns, so a new style was evolved and a much lighter color effect was obtained. Among these later developments, the Iris proved the most successful, the cool and delicate covering under a colorless, transparent glaze giving it a distinction all its own. This was later followed by Vellum ware, a great departure from any known type. Its name gives an idea of its texture and color but fails to convey anything beyond that. It is a transparent mat glaze, soft and close in texture, and greatly enhances the work of the artist, the effect being somewhat similar to the Iris, though much more tender. It is undoubtedly a great ceramic achievement, and when first exhibited at St. Louis in 1904 was pronounced by competent judges to be the only novelty in ceramics in the exhibition. Mat glazes of the known type had been made at Rookwood since 1896, but a mat glaze that should glorify the work of the artist instead of obliterating it was an unknown quantity, and it took much patient investigating and experimenting before it was brought to its present perfection.

A most important work has for the last few years been carried on at Rookwood in the manufacture of tiles for all architectural purposes, and they have to-day perhaps the most extensive palette of mat glaze colors in the world. Wherever it is practical to use a plastic material, either for interior or exterior decoration, the Rookwood artists seem to have anticipated the want, the variety of designs being extremely large. Modeled panels, finished in several soft mat glaze colors, are effectively used in combination with plain tiles of harmonizing shades, and the effect is very soft and subdued—a distinct reproach to the tiles with bright glazes formerly used. Nor is this work by any means confined to flat surfaces, for moldings of all shapes and sizes, curbings and shelves are produced, so that all the details of fireplace and mantel can be constructed in one harmonious whole. The unsightly radiator has even been provided for, which when covered with a grille of pierced tiles becomes a thing of beauty. Many fine hotels and public buildings have rooms entirely decorated with Rookwood productions and these

A MANTEL, BY ROOKWOOD.

will doubtless prove the most lasting monuments to the artistic genius of their creators. The illustrations will give a little idea of the value of these mural decorations, but the quality of the glazes must be seen, for black and white gives no idea of that intangible quality, that spark of life, which are their dominant qualities.

The "unseen forces" who shape Rookwood's destiny and uphold its prestige are too important to be overlooked. W. W. Taylor's fine artistic sense has happily been combined with business acumen, a combination of qualities rarely found, and much of the artistic and commercial success of Rookwood is due to him. To conceive is one thing, to execute quite another, so that Mr. Taylor and the world at large may be congratulated on the association with him of Stanley G. Burt, a thorough ceramist, the maker of those beautiful glazes which have in no small measure contributed to Rookwood's success.

The Rookwood impressed mark, R. P., used since 1886, had a flame added to it in 1887, and an additional one for every year until 1900. Commencing with 1901, the year is added in Roman numerals.

The success of Rookwood naturally evoked a number of imitators, W. A. Long, of Steubenville, being first in the field with what was called Lonhuda ware. The business was sold to S. A. Weller in 1896, Mr. Long continuing in Mr. Weller's employ at his Zanesville pottery. The ware was rechristened Louwelsa, and under Mr. Weller's able management large quantities of it were made. Mr. Weller, with the assistance of two Frenchmen, successfully produced *réflets métalliques*, and some superb specimens were made, but, never learning the secret of its production, it was perforce discontinued when the French workmen left his employment. The Roseville Pottery Co., Zanesville, also produced large quantities of slip-painted ware in the style of Rookwood, and some exquisite color effects in the elusive *sang de boeuf*. This firm has shown considerable initiative in the production of pottery, some carved pieces with Greek designs being good both in spirit and execution. John Herend was the chemist, and to his ability much of the success of the pottery is due. Mr. Herend, we understand, has started a pottery at Golden, Colo., and we may confidently expect that he will continue his previous successes.

Of an entirely different character is the charming green mat glaze pottery of the Grueby Faience Co., Boston. The firm was organized in 1897, and G. P. Kendrick designed the bulk of the shapes. The beautiful softness of the glaze at once brought it into popularity, and an added charm was given it by the simplicity of the ornament where any was employed. The trend of fashion has destroyed the use of vases for merely ornamental purposes, and the firm now bends its energies to the production of tiles and slabs for interior decoration. It was awarded prizes at Paris in 1900 and St. Petersburg in 1901.

The Gates Potteries, of Chicago, makes a mat green glaze known as Teco, similar to the Grueby, and many pieces of mammoth size have been produced. The shapes are quaint and vary considerably from anything else on the market. Some pieces of this mat green had a sheen of silver, which suggested the gilding of refined gold, for the beauty of a mat glaze is the texture and softness, the special quality that appeals to the touch.

NEWCOMBE POTTERY.

Mat glazes are now very generally made, and while they can never go out of fashion, the generally poor shapes clothed with it have done much to destroy its artistic popularity. To these remarks an exception must be made to the work of J. S. Taft & Co., Keene, N. H., their mat glazes equaling anything made either here or abroad.

The Robertsons, of Boston, have successfully produced *sang de boeuf* and also an imitation of the Oriental crackle ware. The works were founded at Chelsea in 1868, and flower pots only were made, but in 1872 the works were enlarged and more pretentious work undertaken, the style of the firm being Chelsea

Keramic Art Works. Imitations of Greek vases and a soft glaze ware decorated with raised flowers were made, and a little later the crackle and *sang de boeuf* were produced by Hugh C. Robertson. The plant was closed in 1888 but reopened in 1891 as the Chelsea Pottery Co., and was afterward moved to Dedham, when the name was again altered, it now being known as the Dedham Pottery Co. Hugh C. Robertson died in 1908, and the business is now conducted by his son, Wm. A. Robertson.

The Sophie Newcombe Memorial College, New Orleans, started a small pottery in 1895, and has evolved a style as original as it is charming. Like a beautiful mat glaze, it never tires the eye, though the effect is obtained by other means. The colors are mostly grays and neutral greens, and the painting being on the biscuit an extreme softness, a restfulness to the eye, and an air of repose results. The subjects are taken exclusively from the local flora, etc., and Professor Woodward may be heartily congratulated on the unequivocal success attained by his pupils.

T. A. Brouwer, Jr., West Hampton, L. I., produces some extremely rich pottery, highly iridescent, which he terms "fire painted," and has also successfully applied gold under the glaze. This is quite effective under a beautiful turquoise glaze if used sparingly.

Mrs. Adelaide Alsop

ROBINEAU WARE.

Robineau, of Syracuse, has within the last few years achieved a remarkable success. Instead of contenting herself with an earthenware body she boldly grappled with the much more difficult porcelain, and has happily succeeded. One by one the technical

LANTERN BY MRS. ROBINEAU.

difficulties of body glaze and color were overcome, and then her fine artistic feeling was brought into play, and with this difficult material she has evolved pieces which are equal to anything made in France, and of which America may be justly proud. A pierced Chinese lantern is a fine example of patient work and technical skill.

Charles Volkmar, Metuchen, N. J., after learning the potter's art in France, started in Brooklyn in 1895, and a little later removed to Corona, N. Y., leaving there in 1902. His early productions included some placques with American subjects in deep blue, and vases, etc., in stoneware. Fortunately he turned his attention to mat glazes, which he now seems to have entirely under control, and with which he produces some charming results. Landscapes in mat glazes do not sound very attractive, and yet with these unwieldly materials he has produced some landscape slabs which are really remarkable for their atmospheric quality. His shapes are always good, and the manufacturing details carefully executed. He is assisted by his son, Leon Volkmar.

Mrs. Frackleton, of Cincinnati; Miss Mary Chase Perry, Detroit; the Marblehead Pottery; Miss Laura H. Osgood, Dayton, O., have all made valuable contributions to American ceramics. It is to this class of worker, rather than the manufacturer, that the credit is due for removing from American pottery the reproach that the industry here had one feature only—the commercial one.

It is by pottery that the intelligence and culture of a nation is most accurately determined in succeeding ages, and perhaps the efforts of these enthusiastic craftsmen may be recognized and their work justly appraised in the future even if it is somewhat neglected to-day.

PLACQUE BY VOLKMAR.

A few words as to American historical pottery may be said here. At the beginning of the nineteenth century English potters issued a number of services, printed in a rich deep blue with American views and (so-called) portraits of her statesmen, which from the large number that have survived must have had a very extensive vogue. They were well engraved and beautifully printed and are now eagerly sought for by collectors. Whilst undoubtedly possessing a certain value the prices paid for some of these pieces seem absurdly above any value they can ever possibly have. The best of these came from Ridgways, Rogers, Edward Wood, James Clews, Stevenson Stubbs, Mayer and others. A little later similar subjects were printed in various colors, pink, black, brown, etc., but neither in the design or the engraving did these begin to compare with the dark blue series. An immense quantity of prints in black on a cream color ware came from Liverpool and are readily distinguished from the Staffordshire pieces. The great popularity attained by these historical pieces created a demand our merchants were not slow to take advantage of, and Jones, McDuffee & Stratton, of Boston; the Rowland and Marsellus Co., New York; Wright, Tyndale & van Roden, Philadelphia, have had a large number of subjects produced, sometimes using the borders made familiar by the old time potters as well as a great number of new ones. In time these subjects, too, will have a certain value, for the old ones being exhausted the collector of the future must need turn to this more modern series. In no case has there been any attempt made to give the impression that these are other than a modern production, the collector being protected by the name of the firm issuing them being plainly marked on the back. The prices obtained for the old blue plates was naturally an incentive to the unscrupulous to produce as near fac simile copies as they could and a good many collectors have been victimized, but they are easily distinguished as the deep blue of the originals has never been successfully reproduced.

OXFORD CHURCH, PHILADELPHIA.　　HONORABLE ARTILLERY PLATE.
　　　　Mercer.　　　　　　　　　　　　Ahrenfeldt.

Apart from this new series of historical plates, from time to time a plate has been considered as the best means of commemorating some particular event, and as only a limited number were issued the future value of these can hardly be realized.

In 1898 the Mercer Pottery Co., Trenton, made a plate commemorative of the Bi-Centenary of the Oxford Church, Philadelphia. The visit of the Honorable Artillery Company of London to the Ancient and Honorable Artillery Company of Boston, in 1904, was distinguished by a souvenir plate issued by Richard Briggs & Co., Boston. It was manufactured by Charles Ahrenfeldt, Limoges. Another successful plate made by the Mercer Pottery Company was the William Penn plate, issued by the Pennsylvania Society of New York, in 1901. The two hundred and fiftieth anniversary of the incorporation of Malden, Mass., in 1899, was marked by issuing a plate which was made

WILLIAM PENN PLATE.   MALDEN PLATE.

for the Richard Briggs Co. by Josiah Wedgwood & Sons. In 1902 the launching of the yacht Meteor was made the occasion for yet another plate executed by the Onondaga Pottery Co., Syracuse.

YACHT METEOR.   WASHINGTON MASONIC PLATE.

Another very fine Mercer Pottery Co. plate is the one issued to commemorate the Sesqui-Centennial of Washington's Initiation

A POTTERY PRIMER.

as a Freemason, 1902. It was designed by George P. Rupp, Librarian of the Grand Lodge of Pennsylvania.

As a matter of fact it has become the custom to mark every event of importance with pottery souvenirs, souvenirs of all conditions of goodness and badness. Perhaps the one most widely distributed was that commemorative of the sinking of the Maine in Havana harbor, issued by the Edwin Bennett Pottery Company, Baltimore. After the Spanish War the market was flooded

UNRECORDED HEROES.

with pottery with portraits in decalcomania of the heroes who participated in it, but perhaps the best one passed almost unnoticed in the hero worship of the moment, for it was a little tribute to the unnamed, the unrecorded heroes, the men behind the guns. It was published by the Baltimore Ceramic Company and the center of it is engraved here for the first time.

With this exception we are indebted to "Old China" for illustrations of these special plates.

THE PHILADELPHIA EXHIBITION.

For many years previous to the Philadelphia Exhibition of 1876, printed dinner ware had been supplanted almost entirely by plain white ware and it was only on the tables of the well-to-do that decorated services were to be seen. We had forgotten the ware of our grandmothers and were content to put up with the heavy white services, the plainness of which was only relieved by an embossed pattern. But this exhibition was the means of calling attention to our backwardness in this respect and the reproach, if reproach it was, was removed. There is no question that this exhibition exerted a more marked influence for good than any ever held here, for then, and then only, the foreign potters sent their very best and latest creations and if in doing so some of their competitors took advantage of the display, the general result was for the good of all, both from an artistic and commercial standpoint.

JERVIS MAT GLAZE POTTERY.

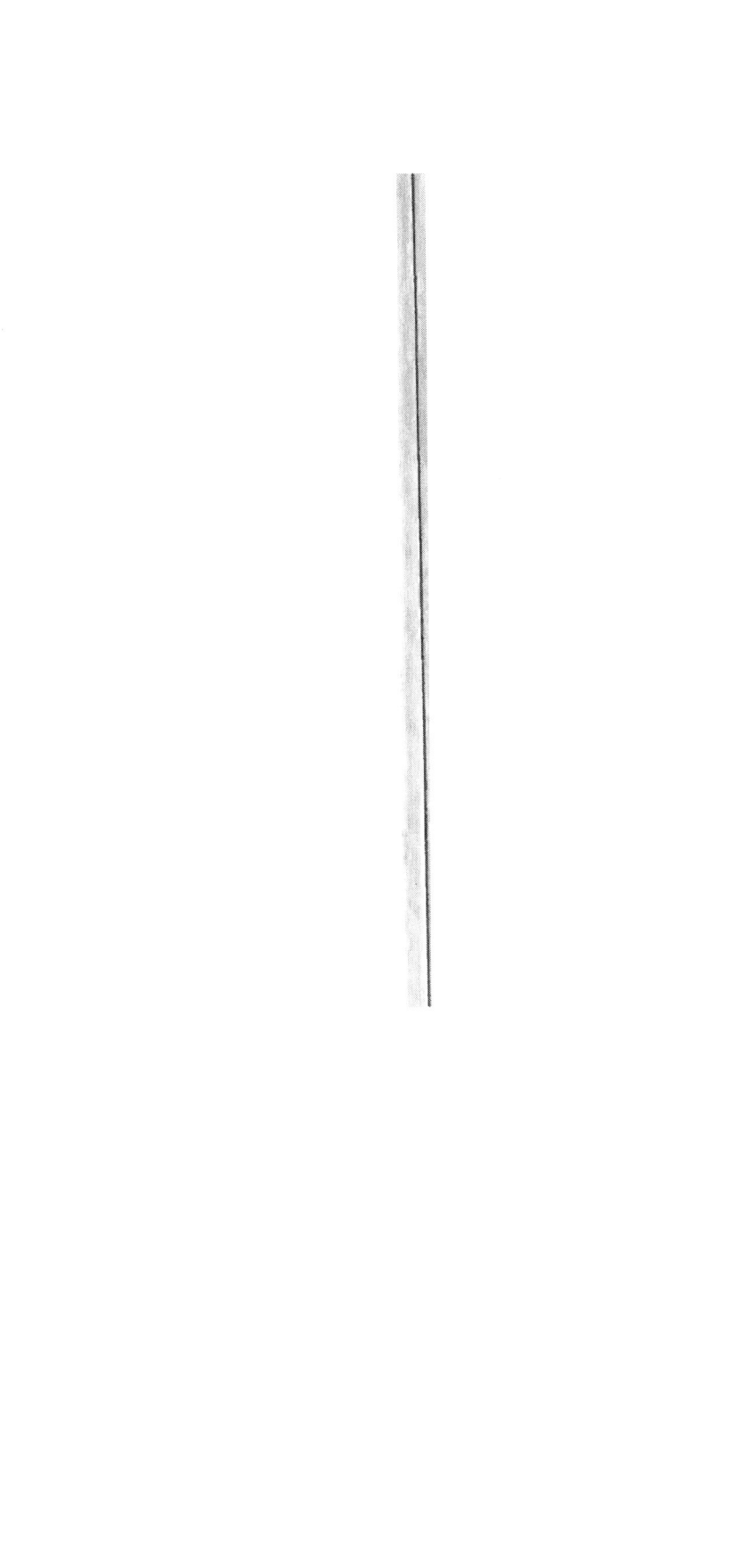

CPSIA information can be obtained
at www.ICGtesting.com
Printed in the USA
BVHW040327020619
549916BV00007B/262/P